Silenced Voices and Extraordinary Conversations

*   *   *

RE-IMAGINING SCHOOLS

Silenced
Voices and
Extraordinary
Conversations

*   *   *

RE-IMAGINING SCHOOLS

Michelle Fine and Lois Weis

Teachers College, Columbia University
New York and London

Published by Teachers College Press, 1234 Amsterdam Avenue, New York, NY 10027

Library of Congress Cataloging-in-Publication Data

Fine, Michelle.
    Silenced voices and extraordinary conversations : re-imagining schools / Michelle Fine and Lois Weis.
        p. cm.
    Includes bibliographical references and index.
    ISBN 0-8077-4284-8 (pbk. : alk. paper) — ISBN 0-8077-4285-6 (cloth : alk. paper)
        1. Educational sociology—United States.   2. Critical pedagogy—United States.   3. School improvement programs—United States.   I. Weis, Lois.   II. Title.
    LC191.4 .F52 2003
    370.11′5—dc21   2002031954

ISBN 0-8077-4284-8 (paper)
ISBN 0-8077-4285-6 (cloth)

Printed on acid-free paper
Manufactured in the United States of America

10   09   08   07   06   05   04   03   8   7   6   5   4   3   2   1

Contents

PART II:
SCENES OF EXTRAORDINARY CONVERSATIONS   109

Acknowledgments

We are left wondering how, at this point in our lives, we can possibly acknowledge all those who have contributed to our writing, thinking, and doing over these past 20 years. Scores of individuals and groups have nurtured our minds, bodies, and souls as we have crafted careers in the midst of the massive abandonment of the public sector. As we struggle, so many others struggle with us, and we are greatly indebted to you. In particular, with respect to this volume, thanks to Carole Saltz, Catherine Bernard, Amy Ferry, Catie LaLonde, Mary Caroll, Michelle Meyers, and all the numerous teachers and students who have worked with us to create educational spaces for "extraordinary conversations." To our families—David, Sam, Caleb; Tereffe, Sara, and Jessica—we love you and thank you, once again, for loving us.

Michelle and Lois
2002

Silenced Voices and Extraordinary Conversations

MICHELLE FINE AND LOIS WEIS

At the dawn of the 21st century, public schools are in a crisis. Their souls are being fought over, with children, especially poor children of color, held hostage to a series of political struggles around vouchers, high-stakes testing, abstinence, evolution, segregation/integration, whole language, bilingualism, governance, and finance (in)equities. Big questions haunt us about the future of public schools, progressive curriculum, student inquiry, performance-based assessments, and teachers as intellectuals. In some ways it is easy for teachers to assume that these are questions for policy makers, legislators, and/or governors—just not for teachers. Just leave us be, they might argue, in our classrooms. With great respect, we disagree. We believe that the future of public education, as an intellectual project of serious, critical engagement, lies in the hands of educators, working with students, parents, community activists, policy makers, and others to re-imagine what could be, and what must be, in those spaces we call schools. Without educators we will have policies that choke, not nurture, the minds we seek to engage, the classes we seek to inspire, the spaces we call schools. Without educators there is likely to be little moral authority in our recognition that schools must challenge the social stratifications of race, ethnicity, and class that currently define, and could destroy, America. As we write, Philadelphia is a battleground for privatization. New Jersey has just passed an abstinence bill that requires educators to present abstinence as the only reliable and preferred form of birth control prior to marriage. The Supreme Court is hearing testimony about Ohio's voucher program. New York City, like other major districts, is suffering a massive shortage of teachers and hiring "emer-

1

gency certified" educators to fill in, disproportionately, in schools of poverty and schools attended predominately by children of color. Laws that require high-stakes testing are transforming the interior life of classrooms, contributing to a spiking of dropout rates throughout the nation.

With this book, we invite teachers into these controversies. We can no longer afford to cede this space to policy makers who know little of the life of a classroom, the curiosity of a child, the moral imperatives of teaching for critical citizenship. We ask teachers to study the strands of schooling that have always been about silencing, defending against what students want to say, refusing to hear about difficult topics, shutting down conversations about sex, dissent, complexity, racism, and the troubling relations of class in America. But, at the same time, we also invite teachers to imagine that it is your responsibility, our responsibility, to fill schools with visions of justice, possibility, and imagination; to engage every child in ways that allow for his or her genius to shine. We ask that you recognize schools as profoundly contradictory spaces and we note that the very spaces of most thrilling pedagogy are always—and even more so today—under threat of being shut down, constrained, controlled, domesticated. We know that preservice teachers, current teachers, and those of us in the university must understand and protect public schools as the only spaces in which all youth—across racial, ethnic, class, legal and (il)legal, sexualities, languages, abilities and (dis)abilities—gather to interrogate the world as it is, and imagine the world as it could be.

That schools inhabit and are even emblematic of contentious public space is no surprise, of course, in a nation in which the "public" is evaporating rapidly. Public housing, parks, libraries, and social services have been stripped to bare bones, while public–private ventures, gentrification, and in some places, vouchers, glide into dominance. Universities are explicitly reliant upon private dollars, and public schools that flourish are now in receipt of private donations, grants, and support from outside the public sphere. The once-clear line separating the public sphere, perhaps always an illusion, has grown increasingly blurry. And yet, in the gentrification of that which is public, schools have retained a sweet loyalty to all. No other public project—except perhaps highways and libraries—are relied upon by everyone. No other institution joins very different bodies, sharing a vision of what is and what could be.

We have no illusions that schools will, in and of themselves, alter the racist and classist structures that dominate America. We recognize painfully that the work of teaching, especially today, cannot be undertaken with a naïve fantasy of creating "extraordinary conversations." We know too well the severe pressures on teachers to produce short-term knowledge for standardized tests that are gates to higher education. And yet we ask you, in this short book, to respond to the voice that "called" you to education; the slice of yourself that seeks to reach the child few have reached, to create a space in a classroom in which difference is interesting, not hierarchical, to imagine that your work as a teacher lies in creating brilliance in the classroom and sanity in the halls of policy making. For too long, policy and practice have been separated. And the price we pay is that policy all but legislates out good educational practice.

This book is an intellectual tour guide to the troubles of bad practice, and the delights of good. We offer this not as a conscience, to instill guilt when you "silence," for you surely will, as we often do. This book is not a tease, to tempt you toward "extraordinary conversations." It is, instead, intended as a nudge to remind us all that schools are profoundly contradictory spaces. They can be repressive and toxic, and they can challenge social (in)justices by opening the doors that race and class hierarchies have glued shut. Schools typically reproduce brutal social stratifications, but occasionally create the very wisdom with youth and by youth that enables and even encourages challenge to social arrangements. Most schools serve as contexts that narrowly constrict identities of youth, but an important exception is that some schools wedge open opportunities for new selves to emerge. It is this latter type that we wish to emphasize here, while at the same time pointing out "what can happen" if intervention does not occur.

Research on schools reflects these same tensions. Some scholars document the mechanisms by which schools reproduce social inequalities—assuring that the "gaps" between racial, ethnic, and social class groups remain or even intensify. These analyses reveal in devastating, fine-grained detail how material inequalities come to be embodied and displayed in youth as "achievement gaps." These writers focus on finance inequities that characterize urban and suburban schools, the uneven distribution of certified teachers, and the insidious schooling policies and practices that track, segregate, silence, punish, and expel youth along the lines of race, ethnicity, class, gender, and sexuality. Much of this research falls theoretically under the umbrella of "repro- duction theory" because it reveals how schools systematically repro- duce the broad-scale inequalities that define America (see Anyon, 1982, 1997; Apple, 1982b; Aronowitz & Giroux, 1993; Banks, 1997; Bowles & Gintis, 1976; Fine, 1992; Grant & Sleeter, 1986; Kozol, 1991; Weis, 1985).

At the same time, many scholars, indeed many of these same scholars, over time have written about schools as potentially liberatory settings; and as sites of social possibility, critical imagination, and individual and collective change (Banks & McGee Banks, 1995; Fine, 1991; Freire, 1970; Giroux, 1983a; Greene, 2001; Ladson-Billings, 1994; McLaren, 1991; Sleeter & Grant, 1994; Weis, 2000). Within this genre of writing, schools constitute sites in which what we call "extraordinary conversations" and practices can flourish, organized toward rigorous academic work and critical democratic engagement of youth and edu- cators (Ayers, Ayers, Dohrn, & Jackson, 2001; Foster, 1997; Meier, 1996). Most often focused on the work of small schools, or "safe" corners within larger ones, these writings allow us to see "what could be" or, perhaps most urgently "what must be" the everyday practice in public education (see Wasley, Fine, Powell, King, Holland, & Gladden, 2000).

This volume, written for current and future educators, takes both of these perspectives seriously. We recognize that in the aggregate schools painfully, systematically, and almost unconsciously reproduce class-, race-, ethnic-, gender-, and sexuality-based inequities rather than challenge them. Urban schools across the nation, especially those that serve poor children and children of color, receive inadequate funding (Kozol, 1991), have a substantially greater percentage of uncredentialed and uncertified teachers (Darling-Hammond, 2001; McNeil, 2000), suffer from decaying, old, and sometimes dangerous physical facilities and, most recently, experience heightened pressures of high-stakes standardized testing, forcing out large numbers of poor and working-class youth prior to graduation from high school (Haney, 1993; McNeil, 2000).

And yet, at the same time, we witness in a series of small schools and pockets within large ones the fact that public schools are the places in which some of the most powerful and compelling work with youth occurs, facilitating individual and collective movements toward social change and social justice (Ayers, Ayers, Dohrn, & Jackson, 2001), stirring personal transformation and political imagination. Educators in urban, suburban, and rural communities, under the best of circumstances and often under the worst, struggle to create classrooms, schools, and communities in which youth engage in critical inquiry, produce rich and provocative conversation, generate significant social projects, and emerge as young scholars with civic and moral sensibilities (Anand, Fine, Perkins, & Surrey, 2002; Meier, 2000).

How do we as researchers, and you as future and present teachers, reconcile these dual/dueling images of public education? For years these two perspectives have run parallel to one another; sometimes they collide; more typically they emerge simply as separate analytic approaches within educational studies.

Silenced Voices and Extraordinary Conversations grapples with both of these perspectives, exploring the explicitly paradoxical nature of public schooling in the United States, in times of enormous public strain and turmoil. We seek to understand and reveal how, when, and with what consequence these coexistent and competing dynamics affect the very nature of schooling in urban America; the teaching and the learning; and the critical analyses of power, consciousness, and identity among urban youth.

This volume is a collection of our essays, crafted over the course of two decades, presented here with a sense of urgency. The essays are arranged so that they begin primarily within this "reproductive" frame, with chapters on silencing, privilege, and schools' refusal to interrupt dominant—and oppressive—voices. You will read quite pronounced "reproductive" tendencies in these early essays that address practices of silencing, triumphant voices of White male privilege, persistent expressions of racism and homophobia. These voices, and these analyses, remain, unfortunately, after 20 years, shamefully current.

The second half of the book moves into sites of what we call "extraordinary conversations," inviting new and veteran educators to imagine and construct with youth classrooms, schools, and communities peppered with questions about power, consciousness, and identity. We have been privileged to work and write with educators who dare to interrogate gender, race, ethnicity, and social class as intellectual and political work; who create very public and also quite subterranean zones in which youth speak critically, analyze collectively, and write toward social possibilities. These are educators who believe, live, and resuscitate democratic commitments of education for all. These latter essays, written with educators and youth workers, reveal the incredible power of classrooms and other educational spaces within schools in which the formerly silenced speak, power inequalities are problematized, and voices of constructive dissent flourish.

By creating a text that juxtaposes extreme instances of the reproduction of social injustice with spaces of amazing talk, we by no means wish to suggest that a good conversation is the same as redistribution of wealth; that progressive curriculum is equivalent to health insurance; that engaging classrooms simply vanish the grotesque inequities that define race, class, gender, and sexuality relations. But neither are we willing to relinquish school as a site irrelevant to powerful and significant social struggle. Perhaps more ambitious, we contend that movements for social justice must work, simultaneously, on questions of social and economic structures and, at the very same time, on critical educational practices in schools and communities, with and for youth.

The essays that follow are designed to help new and current teachers see critically "what is" in schools, to trouble that which is assumed so natural, and to imagine "what could be" (Greene, 2000). You will witness in the text a range of gorgeous secondary-school practices and you will hear knowledge produced by youth whom perhaps you thought weren't capable. From under do-rags and hats, within baggy jeans and from behind teased blond hair, you will marvel as youth create, with educators, intellectual communities in which privilege is denaturalized, identity intersections generously explored, differential opportunity structures examined closely, and new knowledge produced.

Part I "Scenes of Silencing," opens with a set of essays written largely in the 1980s, when we were both immersed in reproduction theory. These essays take up a set of analyses that we still believe to be basically true, arguing that schools are designed and managed, fundamentally, in ways that serve to reproduce and sometimes intensify injustices rooted in class, race, ethnic, gender, and sexuality relations. We document, across five communities in the urban Northeast, how routinely high schools allow, and fail to interrupt, the perpetuation of social inequalities. Drawing from Michelle Fine's 1992 book *Framing Dropouts* and Lois Weis's 1990 text *Working Class Without Work,* we allow the reader to eavesdrop onto what was and, in most large urban high schools (and many suburban ones), what still is. You will hear youths' voices of critique, often muzzled by teachers and other youths eager to "lock down" critical talk in the classroom. You will also hear how the dominant voices of high school often disparage youth of color, girls, and gays and lesbians. That is, in contexts of systemic silencing, there is no vacuum. Instead, the persistent and uninterrupted echoes of damaging voices of privilege populate the halls and the classrooms. Silence is not simply the absence of exported marginalized voices; it is the simultaneous and parasitic invitation to voices that dominate and "other." We warn you—when you finish Part I, you may feel a sense of despair about what is possible within urban secondary schools. But don't put the book down yet!

"Scenes of Extraordinary Conversations," Part II, opens to a set of essays crafted in the 1990s, with public school educators and youth workers with whom we have collaborated. These essays take you into a detracked ninth-grade World Literature course, generated against much community opposition in a desegregated school district; a "girls' group" organized under the auspices of an abstinence-based sex education project, and into a middle school oral history project in which seventh graders learned to be oral historians of the Northern struggle against, and then eventually for, desegregation. In Part II, each essay reveals the crucial and small turns that educators undertake to shelter safe and provocative educational projects, in which power and "difference" are explored, community is built, and education for democracy flourishes. Each essay gives witness to the vibrant, complex, difficult, romantic, and dangerous knowledge and wisdom that urban youth both bring into and can construct within public schools, if only we would listen.

*   *   *

In the Epilogue, we offer up a memo, written to new and veteran educators, opening the lens on what constitutes education, and appreciating how profoundly rich and meaningful sites of democratic education can affect urban youth. We have learned much from youth, including their hunger for intellectual spaces of meaning and engagement. We have learned much from schools; that they can harbor such spaces as exceptions but will rarely commit to buildings filled with engaging practice for all. We have learned much from districts; that they may be willing to "tolerate" a few small schools of possibility, where "excellence" and "equity" sit comfortably side by side, but won't dare to create a district filled with rigorous education for social justice.

But finally, and most important, we have learned from and with youth and educators of courage, that youth only need a tear in the fabric of oppression, and a teacher who believes that education for knowledge and justice is the fundamental work of public schooling. We learned something very wise from one of our educator colleagues, Carlton Jordan: marginalized youth, particularly youth of color, don't expect very much from schools. They don't ask for much, and usually they're not disappointed. But these young men and women know well how to use that momentary contradiction, when a teacher stretches toward, when a classroom comes alive, when brilliance floods the room from all corners. With such a moment, we are delighted to tell you, even the most disengaged youth may just fly.

PART I

Scenes of Silencing

It is likely that Jason Davila will not graduate from high school this year. A senior at South Park High School in Buffalo, New York, Jason has failed the new Math A Regents exam four times. If he fails again on June 15, he won't be allowed to graduate with his class. Jason has a 95 average, an acceptance letter from a well-known local private college, and is ranked 20 in a class of 170 (Cardinale, 2002, p. B–3). Interviewed for the local paper, he asks, "What else could I do?"

The proliferation of increased high-stakes testing means that more students will leave high school without a diploma, at just the moment in history when the presence of a high school diploma is a critical economic litmus test separating the haves from the have nots. While the origins of the "standards movement" may have been systematic accountability, the consequences, at least in the short run, for poor and working-class students are likely to be devastating, with little accompanying positive educational impact. One third of seniors in Buffalo are in danger of not graduating, and this scenario is repeated across the country.

Schooling plays a crucial role in both offering opportunities for individual mobility and, at the same time, reproducing and legitimating large-scale structural inequalities, along the axes of race, ethnicity, class, sexuality, and disability. While the ideology of schooling in the United States is that it offers opportunity to scale the class structure and "transcend" one's home position, this ideology of an "open" class structure means that class positions come to be viewed as largely "deserved." The ideology is thus both deceptive and inviting. We know that many resist this ideology, challenging the beliefs and the practices that obstruct progress for students of color, working-class students, girls, gays and lesbians, and students with disabilities. The struggle over the racial state in the 1950s and 1960s, recent intensified debate over affirmative action on both sides, increased concern for the rights of lesbian and gay students, as well as the educational opportunities related to students with disabilities, and ongoing debate tagged to gender issues and schooling are recent and obvious testimonies to this contest.

Contested, challenged, litigated, resisted as this ideology of meritocracy continues to be, there has been a great deal of work over the past 20 years that demonstrates the ways in which social inequalities are maintained and exacerbated through the institutions of schools. Such work focuses largely on issues of social class, race, and gender and, more recently, sexuality. Many such scholars emphasize the ways in which schools actively prepare students for unequal futures, focusing on teacher-student interaction patterns (Ogbu, 1974; Solomon, 1992), the proliferation of high-stakes testing (Haney, 1993, 2001; McNeil, 2000), tracking and other such segregated educational arrangements (Anyon, 1982, 1997; Locke Davidson, 1996; Oakes, 1985), unequal funding for differentially monied districts (Kozol, 2001), percentage of uncredentialed and uncertified teachers (Darling Hammond, 2001), and the nature of "official" school knowledge that rewards those with middle-class and White cultural capital (Apple, 1982a, 2000; Bernstein, 1977; Bourdieu, 1991; Bourdieu & Passeron, 1977; M.F.D. Young, 1971).

Other scholars, including Paul Willis (1977), Angela McRobbie (1978), Patrick Solomon (1992), Shelbey Steele (1991), and Dorothy Holland and Margaret Eisenhart (1990) argue that inside and through macro structural inequalities grow a series of student cultures, beliefs, practices, engagements, and disengagements forged in relation to unequal social structures that, in the final analysis, ensure that marginalized students remain at the bottom of social hierarchies.

In the 1970s Samuel Bowles and Herbert Gintis (1976) touched off a lively debate regarding the role of schools in the reproduction of the class structure, arguing that education is a crucial element in the reproduction of a division of labor favorable to the maintenance of capitalism. Schools, they believe, reproduce the social relationships necessary to the security of capitalist profits and the stability of the capitalist division of labor. This includes "the patterns of dominance and subordination in the production process, the distribution of ownership among various fragments of the working population—men and women, blacks and whites, and white-collar and blue-collar workers" (p. 126).

While there has certainly been a great deal of engagement with and critique of Bowles and Gintis's ideas, they set the stage for future research around the ways in which schools differentially distribute material opportunities, cultural capital, and notions of presumed place within U.S. society. Schools became, therefore, a key element in the reproduction of an unequal class structure. For Bowles and Gintis, not only does education integrate youth into the economic system "through a structural correspondence between its social relations and those of production" (p. 131), but students learn attitudes and modes of behavior suited to that level in the production process that they will ultimately occupy. Thus, African Americans, for example, are concentrated in schools "whose repressive, arbitrary, generally chaotic internal order, coercive authority structure, and minimal possibility for advancement mirror the characteristics of inferior job situations" (p. 132). Working-class students, across racial and ethnic groups, attend schools that emphasize rule following, and close attention to the specification of others. In sharp contrast, schools in affluent neighborhoods "have relatively open systems that favor student participation, less direct supervision, more student electives, and in general, a value system stressing internalized standards of control" (p. 132).

Bowles and Gintis have been subject to much critical analysis during the past 2 decades (Apple, 1982a; Giroux, 1983a, 1983b, 1991; McCarthy, 1990; McCarthy & Apple, 1988; Ogbu, 1988). Despite these criticisms, however, there is much research to suggest that schools are indeed a site, and continue to be such a site, wherein large-scale structural inequalities are reproduced. What students get in schools does tend to depend on their race, social class, and gender. In addition, as numerous scholars have shown, the formal curriculum is constituted through and with constructed notions of race, social class, gender, able-bodiedness, and appropriate sexuality.

The essays in this section take up these points directly. While neither of us would accept Bowles and Gintis's notions in their entirety, there is a great deal of evidence to suggest that schools, as presently constituted and enacted, do indeed reproduce inequalities—the very inequalities which schools, in the U.S. at least, are ostensibly designed to eliminate. Here we probe carefully the ways in which schools privilege dominant bodies and ideas, while silencing critical, marginal, oppressed and nonhegemonic practices and voices, effectively legitimating those practices and voices which are dominant and serving to knock down others. Through traversing high schools in two communities, we focus on the ways in which our schools serve to etch in inequalities by social class, race, and gender. Jason Davila, whom we met earlier, is not alone here. The question we are left with is this one: Is Jason a "failure" of the system, or has the system "successfully" reproduced race, ethnic, and class hierarchies so that Jason and his friends are systematically ejected from economic, civic, and social struggles for justice? A possible casualty of the educational system, our question must be, What will we—as educators, practitioners, advocates, privileged community members, and parents—do about it?

Silencing and Nurturing Voice in an Improbable Context: Urban Adolescents in Public School

MICHELLE FINE

October 1986, national conference on education: Phyllis Schafly demands that elementary, junior, and senior high school courses on child abuse and incest be banned as "terrorizing tactics against children."

*　　*　　*

Later that same month: Judge Thomas Gray Hull of the Federal District Court in Greeneville, Tennessee upholds Fundamentalist parents' right to remove their children from public school classes in which offending books, including *The Wizard of Oz* and *Diary of a Young Girl*, are taught.

One might wish to imagine that demands for silencing in public schools resonate exclusively from the conservative New Right. In this article, I will argue that Schafly and these Fundamentalist parents

Chapter 1 previously appeared in *Disruptive Voices: The Possibilities of Feminist Research* (pp. 115–138), Ann Arbor: The University of Michigan Press, 1992; and in *Critical Theory and Educational Research*, Peter L. McLaren & James M. Giarelli (Eds.), Albany: State University of New York Press. Used by permission of The University of Michigan Press and the State University of New York Press.

merely caricature what is standard educational practice—the silencing of student and community voices.

Silencing signifies a terror of words, a fear of talk. This chapter examines such practices as they echoed throughout a comprehensive public high school in New York City, in words and in their absence; these practices emanated from the New York City Board of Education, textbook publishers, corporate "benefactors," religious institutions, administrators, teachers, parents, and even students themselves. The essay explores what doesn't get talked about in schools: how "undesirable talk" by students, teachers, parents, and community members is subverted, appropriated, and exported, and how educational policies and procedures obscure the very social, economic, and therefore experiential conditions of students' daily lives while they expel critical "talk" about these conditions from written, oral, and nonverbal expression.

In the odd study of *what's not said* in school, it is crucial to analyze (1) whom silencing protects; (2) the practices by which silencing is institutionalized in contexts of asymmetric power relations; (3) how muting students and their communities systematically undermines a project of educational empowerment (Freire, 1985; Giroux, 1988; Schor, 1980); and (4) how understanding the practices of silencing can make possible a public education that gives voice to students and their communities.

Why silencing in urban public schools? If we believe that city schools are public spheres that promise mobility, equal opportunity, and a forum for participatory democracy (Giroux & McLaren, 1986), indeed one of few such sites were instituted on the grounds of equal access (Carnoy & Levin, 1985); if we recognize the extent to which these institutions nonetheless participate in the very reproduction of class, race, and gender inequities; and if we appreciate that educators working within these schools share a commitment to the former and suffer a disillusionment by the latter, then it can be assumed that the practices of silencing in public schools do the following:

1. Preserve the ideology of equal opportunity and access while obscuring the unequal distribution of resources and outcomes.
2. Create within a system of severe asymmetric power relations the impression of democracy and collaboration among "peers"

(e.g., between White, middle-income school administrators and low-income Black and Hispanic parents or guardians).
3. Quiet student voices of difference and dissent so that such voices, when they burst forth, are rendered deviant and dangerous.
4. Remove from public discourse the tensions between (a) *promises* of mobility and the material *realities* of students' lives; (b) explicit claims to democracy and implicit reinforcement of power asymmetries; (c) schools as an ostensibly *public* sphere and the pollution wrought on them by *private* interests; and (d) the dominant language of equal educational opportunity versus the undeniable evidence of failure as a majority experience of low-income adolescents.

Silencing removes any documentation that all is not well with the workings of the U.S. economy, race and gender relations, and public schooling as the route to class mobility. Let us take a single piece of empirical data provided by the U.S. Department of Labor to understand why urban schools might be motivated to silence.

In 1983, the U.S. Department of Labor published evidence that a high school diploma brings with it quite discrepant opportunities based on one's social class, race, and gender, and further, that the absence of such a diploma ensures quite disparate costs based on the same demographics. Although public rhetoric has assured that dropping out of high school promotes unemployment, poverty, and dependence on crime or welfare, the national data present a story far more complex. Indeed, only 15% of White male dropouts (age 22 to 34) live below the poverty line, compared with 28% of White females, 37% of African-American males, and 62% of African-American females (U.S. Department of Labor, 1983). Further, in a city like New York, dropouts from the wealthiest neighborhoods are more likely to be employed than high school graduates from the poorest neighborhoods (Tobier, 1984). Although having a degree corresponds to employment and poverty levels, this relationship is severely mediated by race, class, and gender stratification.

In the face of these social realities, principals and teachers nevertheless continue to preach, without qualification, to African-American and Hispanic students and parents a rhetoric of equal opportunity and outcomes, the predictive guarantees of a high school diploma, and the invariant economic penalties of dropping out. Although I am no advocate of dropping out of high school, it is clear that silencing—which constitutes the practices by which contradictory evidence, ideologies, and experiences find themselves buried, camouflaged, and discredited—oppresses and insults adolescents and their kin who already "know better."

The press for silencing disproportionately characterizes low-income, minority urban schooling. In these schools, the centralization of the public school administration diminishes community involvement; texts are dated (often 10 to 15 years old) and alienating, in omission and commission; curricula and pedagogies are disempowering, often for students and teachers; strategies for discipline more often than not result in extensive suspension and expulsion rates; and calls for parental involvement often invite bake sale ladies and expel "troublemakers" or advocates. These practices constitute the very means by which schools silence. Self-proclaimed as fortresses against students' communities, city schools offer themselves as "the only way out of Harlem" rather than in partnership with the people, voices, and resources of that community.

Silencing more intimately shapes low-income public schools than relatively privileged ones. In such contexts, there is more to hide and control and, indeed, a greater discrepancy between pronounced ideologies and lived experiences. Further, the luxury of examining the contradictory evidence of social mobility may only be available to those who continue to benefit from existing social arrangements, not those who daily pay the price of social stratification. The dangers inherent in questioning from "above" are minor relative to the dangers presumed inherent in questioning from "below." In low-income schools, then, the process of inquiring into students' lived experience is assumed, a priori, unsafe territory for teachers and administrators. Silencing permeates classroom life so primitively as to render irrelevant the lived experiences, passions, concerns, communities, and biographies of low-income, minority students. In the process, the very voices of these students and their communities, which public education claims to enrich, shut down.

This essay focuses on silencing primarily at the level of classroom and school talk in a low-income, "low-skill" school. Surely there are corporate, governmental, military, and bureaucratic mandates from which demands for silencing derive. But, in the present analysis, these structural demands are assumed, not analyzed. Located primarily within classrooms and with individual teachers, this analysis does not aim to place blame on teachers but only to retrieve from these interactions the raw material for a critical examination of silencing. The data derive from a yearlong ethnography of a high school in Manhattan, attended by 3,200 students, predominantly low-income African Americans and Hispanics from central Harlem and run primarily by African-American paraprofessionals and White teachers (see Fine, 1985, 1986).

An analysis of silencing seems important for two reasons. First, substantial evidence has been accumulated which suggests that many students in this school, considered low in skill, income, and motivation, were quite eager to choreograph their own learning, to generate a curriculum of lived experience, and to engage in a participatory pedagogy (Lather, 1991). Every effort by teachers and administrators which undermined such educational autobiographizing violated one opportunity and probably preempted others, to create dialogue and community—that is, to educate—with students, their kin, and their neighborhoods (Bastian, Fruchter, Gittell, Greer, & Haskins, 1985; Connell, Ashenden, Kessler, & Dowsett, 1982; Lightfoot, 1978). Those administrators, teachers, and paraprofessionals who were sufficiently interested and patient did generate classrooms of relatively "alive" participants. More overwhelming to the observer, however, was the silencing that engulfed life inside most classrooms and administrative offices.

Second, this loss of connection has most significant consequences for low-income minority students. These adolescents are fundamentally ambivalent about the educational process and appropriately cynical about the "guarantees" of an educational credential (Carnoy & Levin, 1985). The linear correspondence of years of education to income does not conform to their reflections on community life. Most were confident that "you can't get nowhere without a diploma." But most were also mindful that "the richest man in my neighborhood didn't graduate but from eighth grade." And, in their lives, both "truths" are defensible. It is precisely by camouflaging such contradictions that educators advance adolescents' cynicism about schooling and credentials, thereby eroding any beliefs in social mobility, community organizing, or the pleasures of intellectual entertainment.

The silencing process is but one aspect of what is often, for low-income students, an impoverished educational tradition. Infiltrating administrative "talk," curriculum development, and pedagogical technique, the means of silencing establish impenetrable barriers between the worlds of school and community life. To unearth the possibility of reclaiming students', teachers', and communities' voices, the practices of silencing must be unpacked.

THE IMPULSE TO SILENCE AS IT SHAPED
EDUCATIONAL RESEARCH

"Lying is done with words and also with silence."
              —Adrienne Rich, *On Lies, Secrets, and Silence*

In June 1984, I began to lay the groundwork for what I hoped would be an ethnography of a public high school in New York City, to begin the fall of 1984 (see Fine 1985, 1986).[1] To my request for entry to his school, the principal greeted me as follows:

Field Note: June, 1984

Mr. Stein: Sure you can do your research on dropouts at this
        school. With one provision. You cannot mention the words
        dropping out to the students.
MF: Why not?
Mr. Stein: If you say it, you encourage them to do it.

Even the research began with a warning to silence me and the imaginations of these adolescents. My field notes continue: "When he said this, I thought, adults should be so lucky, that adolescents wait for us to name the words *dropping out*, or sex, for them to do it." From September through June, witnessing daily life inside the classrooms, deans' and nurses' offices, the attendance room, and the lunchroom, I was repeatedly bewildered that this principal actually believed that adult talk could compel adolescent compliance.

The year progressed. Field notes mounted. What became apparent was a systemic fear of *naming*. Naming involves those practices that facilitate critical conversation about social and economic arrangements, particularly about inequitable distributions of power and resources by which these students and their kin suffer disproportionately. The practices of administration, the relationships between school and community, and the forms of pedagogy and curriculum applied were all scarred by the fear of naming, provoking the move to silence.

THE WHITE NOISE, OR ADMINISTRATIVE SILENCING

Field Note: September, 1984

"We are proud to say that 80 percent of our high school graduates go on to college."
—Principal, Parents' Association meeting, September 1984

At the first Parents' Association meeting, Mr. Stein, the principal, boasted an 80% "college-bound" rate. Almost all graduates of this inner-city high school head for college: a comforting claim oft repeated by urban school administrators in the 1980s. Although accurate, this pronouncement masked the fact that, in this school, as in other comprehensive city high schools, only 20% of the incoming ninth graders *ever* graduate. In other words, only 16% of the 1,220 ninth graders of 1978–79 were headed for college by 1985. The "white noise" of the administration reverberated silence in the audience. Not named, and therefore not problematized, was the substantial issue of low retention rates.

Not naming is an administrative craft. The New York City Board of Education, for example, has refused to monitor retention, promotion, and educational achievement statistics by race and ethnicity for fear of "appearing racist" (personal communication, 1984).[2] Huge discrepancies in educational advancement, by race and ethnicity, thereby remain undocumented in board publications. Likewise, dropout estimates include students on the register when they have not been seen for months; they also presume that students who enroll in general equivalency diploma (GED) programs are not dropouts and that those who produce "working papers" are actually about to embark on careers (which involves a letter, for example, from a Chicken Delight clerk assuring that Jose has a job so that he can leave school at 16). Such procedures contribute to *not naming* the density of the dropout problem.

Although administrative silencing is, unfortunately, almost a redundancy, the concerns of this essay are primarily focused on classroom- and school-based activities of silencing. By no means universal, the fear of naming was nevertheless commonplace, applied at this school by conservative and liberal educators alike. Conservative administrators and teachers viewed most of their students as unteachable. It was believed, following the logic of social studies teacher Mr. Rosaldo, that, "if we save 20 percent, that's a miracle. Most of these kids don't have a chance." For these educators, naming social and economic inequities in their classrooms would only expose circumstances they believed to be self-imposed. Perhaps these teachers themselves had been silenced over time. It is worth noting that correlational evidence (Fine, 1983) suggests that educators who feel most disempowered in their institutions are most likely to believe that "these kids can't be helped" and that those who feel relatively empowered are likely to believe that they "can make a difference in the lives of these youths."

Disempowered and alienated themselves, such educators see an enormous and inherent distance between "them" and "us," a distance, whether assumed biological or social, which could not be bridged by the mechanics of public schooling. So, when I presented "dropout data" to these faculty members and suggested that the level of involuntary "discharges" processed through this school would never be tolerated in the schools attended by their children, I was rapidly chastised: "That's an absurd comparison. The schools my kids go to are nothing like this—the comparison is sensationalist!" The social distance between them and us is reified and naturalized. Naming would only be inciting.

The more liberal position of other educators, for whom not naming was also routine, involved their loyalty to believe in a color- and class-neutral meritocracy. These educators dismissed the very empirical data that would have informed the naming process. Here they followed the logic of science teacher Ms. Tannenbaum: "If these students work hard, they can really become something. Especially today with affirmative action." They rejected counterevidence: for example, that African-American high school graduates living in Harlem are still far less likely to be employed than White high school dropouts living in more elite sections of New York (Tobier, 1984), for fear that such data would "discourage students from hard work and dreams." Enormous energy must be required to sustain beliefs in equal opportunity and the colorblind power of credentials and to silence nagging losses of faith when evidence to the contrary compels on a daily basis. Naming in such a case would only unmask realities, fundamentally disrupting or contradicting educators' and presumably students' belief systems.

Still other educators actively engaged their students in lively, critical discourse about the complexities and inequities of prevailing economic and social relations. Often importing politics from other spheres of their lives, the feminist English teacher, the community activist who taught grammar, or the Marxist historian wove critical analysis into their classrooms, with little effort. These offices and classrooms were permeated with the openness of naming, free of the musty tension that derives from conversations-not-had.

Most educators at this school, however, seemed to survive by not naming or analyzing social problems. They administered and taught in ways that established the school as a fortress for mobility *out* of the students' communities. They taught with curricular and pedagogical techniques they hoped would soothe students and smooth social contradictions. Many would probably have not considered conversation about social class, gender, or race politics relevant to their courses or easily integrated into their curricula. Some would argue that inclusion of these topics would be "political"—whereas exclusion was not. One could have assumed that they benignly neglected these topics.

But evidence of educators' *fear*, rather than *neglect*, grew apparent when students (activated by curiosity and rebellion) initiated conversations of critique which were rapidly dismissed. A systemic expulsion of dangerous topics permeated these classrooms. For educators to examine the very conditions that contribute to social class, racial, ethnic, and gender stratification in the United States, when they are relatively privileged by class usually and race often, seemed to introduce fantasies of danger, a pedagogy that would threaten, rather than protect, teacher control. Such conversations would problematize what seem like "natural" social distinctions, potentially eroding teachers' authority. If not by conscious choice, then, some teachers and administrators actively engaged in pedagogical strategies that preempted, detoured, or ghettoized such conversations. Not naming, as a particular form of silencing, was accomplished creatively. Often with good intentions, the practice bore devastating consequences.

Naming indeed subverts or complicates those beliefs that public schools aim to promote. It is for this very reason essential that naming be inherent in the educational process, in the creation of an empowered and critical constituency of citizens (Aronowitz & Giroux, 1985). It was ironic to note that pedagogic and curricular attempts to not name or to actively avoid such conversation indeed cost teachers control over their classrooms. Efforts to shut down such conversations were usually followed by the counting of money by males, the application of mascara or lipstick by females, and the laying down of heads on desks by students of both genders: the loss of control over the classroom.

To not name bears consequences for all students, but most dramatically for low-income, minority youths. To not name systematically alienates, cuts off from home, from heritage, and from lived experience and, ultimately, severs these students from their educational process. The pedagogical and curricular strategies employed in not naming are examined critically below.

PEDAGOGICAL AND CURRICULAR
MUTING OF STUDENTS' VOICES

Constructing Taboo Voices: Conversations Never Had

A mechanistic view of teachers terrorized by naming and students passively accommodating could not be further from the daily realities of life inside a public high school. Many teachers name and critique, although most don't. Some students passively shut down, although most remain alive and even resistant. Classrooms are filled with students wearing Walkmans, conversing among themselves and with friends in the halls, and some even persistently challenging the experiences and expertise of their teachers. But the typical classroom still values silence, control, and quiet, as Jean Anyon (1983), John Goodlad (1984), Theodore Sizer (1985), and others have documented. The insidious push toward silence in low-income schools became most clear sometime after my interview with Eartha, a 16-year-old high school dropout.

Field Note: January 24

MF: Eartha, when you were a kid, did you participate a lot in school?
Eartha: Not me, I was a good kid. Made no trouble.

I asked this question of 55 high school dropouts. After the third responded as Eartha did, I realized that, for me, participation was encouraged, delighted in, and a measure of the "good student." Yet, for these adolescents, given their histories of schooling, participation meant poor discipline and rude classroom behavior.

Students learn the dangers of talk, the codes of participating and not, and they learn, in more nuanced ways, which conversations are never to be had. In Philadelphia, a young high school student explained to me: "We are not allowed to talk about abortion. They tell us we can't discuss it no way." When I asked a school district administrator about this policy, she qualified: "It's not that they can't *talk* about it. If the topic is raised by a student, the teacher can define abortion, just not discuss it beyond that." The distinction between defining and discussing makes sense only if learning assumes teacher authority, if pedagogy requires single truths, and if classroom control implies silence. Perhaps this is why classroom control often feels so fragile. Control through omission *is* fragile. Fully contingent on students' willingness to collude, such control betrays a plea for student compliance.

Silencing in public schools comes in many forms. Conversations can be closed by teachers or forestalled by student collusion. But other conversations are expressly withheld, never had. Such a policy of enforced silencing was applied to information about the severe economic and social consequences of dropping out of high school. This information was systematically withheld from students who were being discharged. Few, as a consequence, ever entertained second thoughts.

When students are discharged in New York State, they are guaranteed an exit interview, which, in most cases I observed, involved an attendance officer who asked students what they planned to do and then requested a meeting with the parent or guardian to sign official documents. The officer handed the student a list of GED and outreach programs. The student left, often eager to find work, get a GED, go to a private business school, or join the military. Informed conversations about the consequences of the students' "decision" were not legally mandated. As they left, these adolescents *did not learn* the following:

- Over 50% of African-American high school dropouts suffer unemployment in cities like New York City (U.S. Commission on Civil Rights, 1982).
- Forty-eight percent of New Yorkers who sit for the graduate equivalency diploma test fail (New York State Department of Education, 1985).
- Private trade schools, including cosmetology, beautician, and business schools, have been charged with unethical recruitment practices, exploitation of students, earning more from students who drop out than those who stay, not providing promised jobs, and having, on average, a 70% dropout rate (see Fine, 1986).
- The military, during "peacetime," refuses to accept females with no high school degree and only reluctantly accepts males, who suffer an extreme less-than-honorable discharge rate within 6 months of enlistment (Militarism Resource Project, 1985).

Students who left high school prior to graduation were thereby denied informed consent. Conversations-not-had nurtured powerful folk beliefs among adolescents: that "the GED is no sweat, a piece of cake"; that "you can get jobs, they promise, after goin' to Sutton or ABI [American Business Institute]"; or that "in the army, I can get me a GED, skills, travel, benefits." Such is a powerful form of silencing.

Closing Down Conversations

Field Note: October 17, Business Class

White Teacher: What's EOE?
African-American Male Student: Equal over time.
White Teacher: Not quite. Anyone else?
African-American Female Student: Equal Opportunity Employer.
Teacher: That's right.
African-American Male Student (2): What does that mean?
Teacher: That means that an employer can't discriminate on the basis of sex, age, marital status, or race.

African-American Male Student (2): But wait, sometimes White
   people only hire White people.
Teacher: No, they're not supposed to if they say EOE in their
   ads. Now take out your homework.

Later that day:
MF (to teacher): Why don't you discuss racism in your class?
Teacher: It would demoralize the students, they need to feel positive and optimistic—like they have a chance. Racism is
   just an excuse they use to not try harder.

What enables some teachers to act as if students benefit from such
smoothing over (Wexler, 1983)? For whose good are the roots, the
scars, and the structures of class, race, and gender inequity obscured
by teachers, texts, and tests (Anyon, 1983)? Are not the "fears of
demoralizing" a projection by teachers of their own silenced loss of
faith in public education and their own fears of unmasking or freeing
a conversation about social inequities?

At the level of curriculum, texts, and conversation in classrooms,
school talk and knowledge were radically severed from the daily
realities of adolescents' lives and more systematically aligned with the
lives of teachers (McNeil, 1981). Routinely discouraged from critically
examining the conditions of their lives, dissuaded from creating their
own curriculum, built of what they know, students were often encouraged to disparage the circumstances in which they live, warned by
their teachers: "You act like that, and you'll end up on welfare!" (Most
were or had been surviving on some form of federal, state, or city
assistance.)

"Good students" therefore managed these dual/duel worlds by
learning to speak standard English dialect, whether they originally
spoke Black English, Spanish, or Creole. More poignant still, they
trained themselves to produce two voices. One's "own" voice alter-
nated with an "academic" voice. The latter denied class, gender, and
race conflict; repeated the words of hard work, success, and their
"natural" sequence; and stifled any desire to disrupt.

In a study conducted in 1981, it was found that the group of South
Bronx students who were "successes"—those who remained in high
school—when compared with dropouts, were significantly more depressed, less politically aware, less likely to be assertive in the class-

room if they were undergraded, and more conformist (Fine, 1991). A moderate level of depression, an absence of political awareness, and a persistence of self-blame, low assertiveness, and high conformity may tragically have constituted the "good" urban student at this high school. They learned not to raise, and indeed to help shut down, "dangerous" conversation. The price of success may have been muting one's own voice.

Other students from the school in Manhattan resolved the "two voices" tension with creative, if ultimately self-defeating, strategies. Cheray reflected on the hegemonic academic voice after she dropped out: "In school, we learned Columbus Avenue stuff, and *I* had to translate it into Harlem. They think livin' up here is unsafe and our lives are so bad. That we should want to move out and get away. That's what you're supposed to learn." Tony thoroughly challenged the academic voice as ineffective pedagogy: "I never got math when I was in school. Then I started sellin' dope and runnin' numbers, and I picked it up right away. They should teach the way it matters." Alicia accepted the academic voice as the standard, while disparaging with faint praise her own voice: "I'm *wise* but not *smart*. There's a difference. I can walk into a room, and I know what people be thinkin' and what's goin' down. But not what he be talkin' about in history."

Finally, many saw the academic voice as the exclusively legitimate, if inaccessible, mode of social discourse. Monique, after 2 months out of school, admitted: "I'm scared to go out lookin' for a job. They be usin' words in the interview like in school. Words I don't know. I can't be askin' them for a dictionary. It's like in school. You ask and you feel like a dummy."

By segregating the academic voice from students' own voices, public schools do not only linguistic violence (Zorn, 1982). The intellectual, social, and emotional substance that constitutes minority students' lives in this school was routinely treated as irrelevant, to be displaced and silenced. Their responses, spanning acquiescence to resistance, bore serious consequences.

CONTRADICTIONS FOLDED: EXCLUDING "REDUNDANT" VOICES

If "lived talk" was actively expelled on the basis of content, contradictory talk was basically rendered impossible. Social contradictions were folded into dichotomous choices. What does this obscure, and whom does this accommodate? The creation of such dichotomies and the reification of single truths may bolster educators' authority, reinforcing the distance between those who *know* and those who *don't*, often discrediting those who *think* in complexity (McNeil, 1981).

To illustrate: In early spring, a social studies teacher structured an in-class debate on Bernard Goetz—New York City's "subway vigilante." She invited "those students who agree with Goetz to sit on one side of the room and those who think he was wrong to sit on the other side." To the large residual group who remained mid-room, the teacher remarked, "Don't be lazy. You have to make a decision. Like at work, you can't be passive." A few wandered over to the "pro-Goetz" side. About six remained in the center. Somewhat angry, the teacher continued: "OK, first we'll hear the pro-Goetz side and then the anti-Goetz side. Those of you who have no opinions, who haven't even thought about the issue, you won't get to talk unless we have time."

Deidre, an African-American senior, bright and always quick to raise contradictions otherwise obscured, advocated the legitimacy of the middle group. "It's not that I have no opinions. I don't like Goetz shootin' up people who look like my brother, but I don't like feelin' unsafe in the projects or in my neighborhood either. I got lots of opinions. I ain't bein' quiet cause I can't decide if he's right or wrong. I'm talkin'." Deidre's comment legitimized for herself and others the right to hold complex, perhaps even contradictory, positions on a complex situation. Such legitimacy was rarely granted by faculty—with clear and important exceptions, including activist faculty and those paraprofessionals who lived in central Harlem with the kids, who understood and respected much about their lives.

Among the chorus of voices heard within this high school, then, lay little room for Gramsci's (1971) contradictory consciousness. Artificial dichotomies were delivered as natural: right and wrong answers, appropriate and inappropriate behavior, moral and immoral people, dumb and smart students, responsible and irresponsible parents, good and bad neighborhoods. Contradiction and ambivalence, forced underground, were experienced often, if expressed rarely.

I asked Ronald, a student in remedial reading class, why he stayed in school. He responded with sophistication and complexity: "Reason I stay in school is 'cause every time I get on the subway I see this drunk and I think 'not me.' But then I think 'bet he has a high school degree.'" The power of his statement lies in its honesty, as well as the infrequency with which such comments were voiced. Ronald explained that he expected support for this position neither in school nor on the street. School talk promised what few believed but many repeated: that hard work and education breed success and a guarantee against welfare. Street talk belied another reality, described by Shondra: "They be sayin', 'What you doin' in school? Could be out here scramblin' [selling drugs] and makin' money now. That degree ain't gonna get you nothing better.'"

When African-American adolescent high school graduates, in the October following graduation, suffered a 56% unemployment rate and African-American adolescent high school dropouts suffered a 70% unemployment rate, the very contradictions that were amplified in the minds and worries of these young men and women remained unspoken within school (Young, 1983).

CONVERSATIONS PSYCHOLOGIZED: SPLITTING THE PERSONAL AND THE SOCIAL VOICE

Some conversations within schools were closed; others were dichotomized. Yet a few conversations, indeed those most relevant to inequitable social arrangements, remained psychologized: managed as personal problems inside the offices of school psychologists or counselors. The lived experiences of *all* adolescents, and particularly those surviving city life in poverty, place their physical and mental well-being as well as that of their kin in constant jeopardy. And yet conversations about these very conditions of life, about alcoholism, drug abuse, domestic violence, environmental hazards, gentrification, and poor health—to the extent that they happened at all—remained confined to individual sessions with counselors (for those lucky enough to gain hearing with a counselor in the 800 : 1 ratio and gutsy enough to raise the issue) or, if made academic, were raised in hygiene class (for those fortunate enough to have made it to 12th grade, when hygiene was offered). A biology teacher, one of the few African-American teachers in the school, actually integrated creative writing assignments such as "My life as an alcoholic" and "My life as a child of an alcoholic" into her biology class curriculum. Her department chairman reprimanded her severely for introducing "extraneous materials." Teachers, too, were silenced.

The marginalizing of the health and social problems experienced by these adolescents exemplified the systematic unwillingness to address these concerns academically, in social studies, science, English, or even math. A harsh resistance to name the lived experiences of these teens paralleled the unwillingness to integrate these experiences as the substance of learning. Issues to be avoided at all costs, they were addressed psychologically, individually, and in isolation and, even then, only after they pierced the life of the adolescent seeking help.

The offices of school psychologists or counselors therefore became the primary sites for addressing what were indeed social concerns, should have been academic concerns, and were most likely to be managed as personal and private concerns. The privatizing and psychologizing of public and political issues served to reinforce the alienation of students' lives from their educational experience.

DEMOCRACY AND DISCIPLINE: MAINTAINING SILENCE BY APPROPRIATING AND EXPORTING DISSENT

The means of maintaining silences and ensuring no dangerous disruptions know few bounds. If silence masks asymmetric power relations, it also ensures the impression of democracy for parents and students by appropriating and exporting dissent. This strategy has gained popularity in the fashionable times of "empowerment."

At this school, the Parents' Association executive board was composed of ten parents: eight African-American women, one African-American man, and one White woman. Eight no longer had children attending the school. At about mid-year, teachers were demanding smaller class size. So, too, was the president of the Parents' Association at this executive meeting with the principal.

> *President*: I'm concerned about class size. Carol Bellamy (city council president) notified us that you received monies earmarked to reduce class size, and yet what have you done?
>
> *Mr. Stein*: Quinones [school's chancellor] promised no high school class greater than 34 by February. That's impossible!

What he is asking I can't guarantee, unless *you* tell me
what to do. If I reduce class size, I must eliminate all
specialized classes, all electives. Even then I can't guarantee. To accede to Quinones, that classes be less than 34, we
must eliminate the elective in English, Social Studies, all art
classes, 11th-year Math, Physics, accounting, word process-
ing. We were going to offer a Haitian Patois Bilingual program, fourth-year French, a Museums program, Bio-
Pre-Med, Health Careers, Coop and Pre-Coop, Choreography, and Advanced Ballet. The nature of the school will be
changed fundamentally. We won't be able to call this an
academic high school, only a program for slow
learners.

Woman: (1): Those are very important classes.

Mr. Stein: I am willing to keep these classes. Parents want me
to keep these classes. That's where I'm at.

Woman (2): What is the average?

Mr. Stein: 33.

Woman (1): Are any classes over 40?

Mr. Stein: No, except if it's a *singleton* class—the only one offered. If these courses weren't important, we wouldn't
keep them. You know we always work together. If it's
your feeling we should not eliminate all electives and maintain things, OK! Any comments?

Woman (1): I think continue. Youngsters aren't getting enough
now. And the teachers will not teach any more.

Woman (3): You have our unanimous consent and support.

Mr. Stein: When I talk to the Board of Education, I'll say I'm
talking for the parents.

Woman (4): I think it's impossible to teach 40.

Mr. Stein: We have a space problem. Any other issues?

An equally conciliatory student council was constituted to decide
on student activities, prom arrangements, and student fees. The council was largely pleased to meet in the principal's office. At the level
of critique, silence was guaranteed by the selection and then the invited
"democratic participation" of these parents and students.

If dissent was appropriated through mechanisms of democracy,
it was exported through mechanisms of discipline. The most effective

procedure for silencing was to banish the source of dissent, tallied in the school's dropout rate. As indicated by the South Bronx study referred to above (Fine, 1983) and the research of others (Elliott, Voss, & Wendling, 1966; Felice, 1981; Fine & Rosenberg, 1983), it is often the academic critic resisting the intellectual and verbal girdles of schooling who "drops out" or is pushed out of low-income schools. Extraordinary rates of suspensions, expulsions, and discharges experienced by African-American and Hispanic youths speak to this form of silencing (Advocates for Children, 1985). Estimates of urban dropout rates range from approximately 42% from New York City, Boston, and Chicago boards of education to 68 to 80% from Aspira (1983), an educational advocacy organization.

At the school that served as the site for this ethnographic research, a 66% dropout rate was calculated. Two thirds of the students who began ninth grade in 1978–79 did not receive diplomas or degrees by June 1985. I presented these findings to a collection of deans, advisors, counselors, administrators, and teachers, many of whom were the sponsors and executors of the discharge process. At first I met with total silence. A dean then explained, "These kids need to be out. It's unfair to the rest. My job is like a pilot on a hijacked plane. My job is to throw the hijacker overboard." The one African-American woman in the room, a guidance counselor, followed: "What Michelle is saying is true. We do throw students out of here and deny them their education. Black kids especially." Two White male administrators interrupted, chiding what they called the "liberal tendencies" of guidance counselors, who "don't see how really dangerous these kids are." The meeting ended.

Dissent was institutionally "democraticized," exported, trivialized, or bureaucratized. These mechanisms made it unlikely for change or challenge to be given a serious hearing.

WHISPERS OF RESISTANCE: THE SILENCED SPEAK

In low-income public high schools organized around control through silence, the student, parent, teacher, or paraprofessional who talks, tells, or wants to speak transforms rapidly into the subversive, the troublemaker. Students, unless they spoke in an honors class or affected the academic mode of introducing nondangerous topics and benign words—if not protected by wealth, influential parents, or an unusual capacity to be critics *and* good students—emerged as provocateurs. Depending on school, circumstances, and style, students' responses to such silencing varied. Maria buried herself in mute isolation. Steven organized students against many of his teachers. Most of these youths, for complex reasons, ultimately fled prior to graduation. Some then sought "alternative contexts" in which their strengths, competencies, and voices could flourish on their own terms:

> *Hector's a subway graffiti artist*: "It's like an experience you never get. You're on the subway tracks. Its 3 a.m., dark, cold, and scary. You're trying to create your best. The cops can come to bust you, or you could fall on the electric third rail. My friend died when he dropped his spray paint on that rail. It exploded. He died and I watched. It's awesome, intense. A peak moment when you can't concentrate on nothin', no problems, just creation. And it's like a family. When Michael Stewart [graffiti artist] was killed by cops, you know he was a graffiti man, we all came out of retirement to mourn him. Even me, I stopped 'cause my girl said it was dangerous. We came out and painted funeral scenes and cemeteries on the LL #1 and the N [subway lines]. For Michael. We know each other; you know an artist when you see him. It's a family. Belonging. They want me in, not out, like at school."
>
> *Carmen pursued the Job Corps when she left school*: "You ever try plastering, Michelle? It's great. You see holes in walls. You see a problem and you fix it. Job Corps lost its money when I was in it, in Albany. I had to come home, back to Harlem. I felt better there than ever in my school. Now I do nothin'. It's a shame. Never felt as good as then."
>
> *Monique got pregnant and then dropped out*: "I wasn't never good at nothing. In school I felt stupid and older than the rest. But I'm a great mother to Chita. Catholic schools for my baby, and maybe a house in New Jersey."
>
> *Carlos, who left school at age 20, after 5 frustrating years since he and his parents exiled illegally from Mexico, hopes to join the military*: "I don't want to kill nobody. Just, you know how they advertise, the Marines. I never been one of a Few and the Proud. I'm always 'shamed of myself. So I'd like to try it."

In an uninviting economy, these adolescents responded to the silences transmitted through public schooling by pursuing what they considered to be creative alternatives. But let us understand that, for such low-income youths, these alternatives generally *replace* formal schooling. Creative alternatives for middle-class adolescents, an after-school art class or music lessons privately afforded by parents, generally *supplement* formal schooling.

Whereas school-imposed silence may be an initiation to adulthood for the middle-class adolescent about to embark on a life of participation and agency, school-imposed silence more typically represents the orientation to adulthood for the low-income or working-class adolescent about to embark on a life of work at McDonalds, in a factory, as a domestic or clerical, and/or on Aid to Families with Dependent Children (AFDC). For the low-income student, the imposed silences of high school cannot be ignored as a necessary means to an end. They are the present, *and* they are likely to be the future (Ogbu, 1978).

Some teachers, paraprofessionals, parents, and students expressly devoted their time, energy, and classes to exposing silences institutionally imposed. One reading teacher prepared original grammar worksheets, including items such as "Most women in Puerto Rico (is, are) oppressed." A history teacher dramatically presented his autobiography to his class, woven with details on the life of Paul Robeson. An English teacher formed a writer's collective of her multilingual "remedial" writing students. A paraprofessional spoke openly with students who decided not to report the prime suspect in a local murder to the police but to clergy instead. She recognized that their lives would be in jeopardy, despite "what the administrators who go home to the suburbs preach." But these voices of naming were weak, individual, and isolated.

What if these voices, along with the chorus of dropouts, were allowed expression? If they were not whispered, isolated, or drowned out in disparagement, what would happen if these stories were solicited, celebrated, and woven into a curriculum? What if the history of schooling were written by those high school critics who remained in school and those who dropped out? What if the "dropout problem" were studied in social studies as a collective critique by consumers of public education?

Dropping out, or other forms of critique, are viewed instead by educators, policy makers, teachers, and often students as individual acts, expressions of incompetence or self-sabotage. As alive, motivated, and critical as they were at age 17, most of the interviewed dropouts were silenced, withdrawn, and depressed by age 22. They had tried the private trade schools, been in and out of the military, failed the GED exam once or more, had too many children to care for, too many bills to pay, and only self-blaming regrets, seeking private solutions to public problems. Muting, by the larger society, had ultimately succeeded, even for those who fled initially with resistance, energy, and vision (Apple, 1982b).

I'll end with an image that occurred throughout the year, repeated across classrooms and across urban public high schools. As familiar as it is haunting, the portrait most dramatically captures the physical embodiment of silencing in urban schools.

Field Note: February 16

Patrice is a young African-American female, in 11th grade. She says nothing all day in school. She sits perfectly mute. No need to coerce her into silence. She often wears her coat in class. Sometimes she lays her head on her desk. She never disrupts. Never disobeys. Never speaks. And is never identified as a problem. Is she the student who couldn't develop two voices and so silenced both? Is she so filled with anger, she fears to speak? Or so filled with depression, she knows not what to say?

Whose problem is Patrice?

NURTURING THE POSSIBILITY OF VOICE
IN AN IMPROBABLE CONTEXT

To pose a critique of silencing requires a parallel commitment to exploring the possibility of voice in public schools. For, if we are to abandon all hopes that much can be done inside the public school system, we have surely and irretrievably sealed and silenced the fates of children and adolescents like those described in this chapter. And so the responsibility to unearth possibility lies with the critic of educational institutions (Aronowitz & Giroux, 1985).

Indeed, after a year at this public school, I left with little but optimism about these youngsters and little but pessimism about public high schools as currently structured. And yet it would be inauthentic not to note the repeated ways in which students, communities, and parents were, and the more numerous ways in which they could be, granted voice inside schools. Those teachers who imported politics from elsewhere, who recognized that educational work is political work that to talk about or not to talk about economic arrangements is to do political work, took as their individual and collective responsibility a curriculum that included critical examination of social and economic issues and a pedagogy that attended to the multiple perspectives and ideas inside their classrooms. In vocational education class, Ms. Rodriquez invited students to discuss the conditions of their lives, the relationship of labor market opportunities to their own and their families' survival, and the consequences of giving up, being discouraged, or making trouble at work. Although a thoroughgoing critique of workplace management was not undertaken, a surface analysis was begun, and trust was enabled. Likewise, in hygiene, Ms. Wasserman continually probed the lived experiences and diversity among the students. She integrated writing assignments with curricular and social issues, inviting students to author letters to their mothers—alive or dead—about questions "you wish you could or did ask her about sexuality, marriage, and romance." A social studies teacher created a class assignment in which students investigated their communities, conducting oral histories with neighbors, shop owners, and local organizers to map community life historically and currently.

But, of course, much more could be done if all educators saw politics as inherent and the giving of voice as essential to the task of education. To *not* mention racism is as political a stance as is a thoroughgoing discussion of its dynamics; to *not* examine domestic violence bears consequences for the numerous youths who have witnessed abuse at home and feel alone, alienated in their experience, unable to concentrate, so that the effects of the violence permeate the classroom even—or particularly—if not named.

I am not asking teachers to undertake therapy in the classroom nor to present only one political view but, instead, to interrogate the very conditions of students' lives and the very thoughts that they entertain as the "stuff" of schooling.

The good news is that students in public high schools, as thoroughly silenced as they may be, retain the energy, persistence, and even resistance that fuel a willingness to keep trying to get a hearing.

They probe teachers they don't agree with, challenge the lived experiences of these authorities, and actively spoof the class and race biases that routinely structure classroom activities:

Field Note: September 18

Social Studies Teacher: A few years ago a journalist went through Kissinger's garbage and learned a lot about his life. Let's make believe we are all sanitation men going through rich people's and poor people's garbage. What would we find in rich people's garbage?

Students call out: Golf club! Polo stick! Empty bottle of Halston! Champagne bottle! Alimony statements! Leftover caviar! Receipts from Saks, Barneys, Bloomies! Old business and love letters! Rarely worn shoes—They love to spend money! Bills from the plastic surgeon—for a tummy tuck! Things that are useful that they just throw out 'cause they don't like it! Rich people got ulcers, so they have lots of medicine bottles!

Teacher: Now, the poor man's garbage. What would you find?

Student (1): Not much, we're using it.

Student (2): Holey shoes.

Others: Tuna cans! Bread bags!

Student (3): That's right, we eat a lot of bread!

Others: USDA cheese boxes! Empty no-frills cans! Woolworth receipts! Reused items from rich man's garbage! *Daily News*!

Student (3): *Daily News* from week before.

Others: Old appliances! Rusty toasters!

Student (4): Yeah, we eat lots of burned toast.

Student (5): You know, poor people aren't unhappy. We like being poor.

Teacher: Let's not get into value judgments now. There are people who are eccentric and don't have these things, and poor people who have luxuries, so it is hard to make generalizations.

Student (6): That's why we're poor!

Despite the teacher's attempts to halt the conversation of critique, these students initiated and persisted. The room for possibility lies with the energy of these adolescents and with those educators who are creative and gutsy enough to see as their job, their passion, and their responsibility the political work of educating toward a voice.

POSTSCRIPT ON RESEARCH AS EXPOSING
THE PRACTICES OF SILENCING

The process of conducting research within schools to identify words that could have been said, talk that should have been nurtured, and information that needed to be announced suffers from voyeurism and perhaps the worst of post hoc academic arrogance. The researcher's sadistic pleasure in spotting another teacher's collapsed contradiction, aborted analysis, or silencing sentence was moderated only by the ever-present knowledge that similar analytic surgery could easily be performed on my own classes.

And yet it is the very naturalness of not naming, of shutting down or marginalizing conversations for the "sake of getting on with learning" that demands educators' attention, particularly so for low-income youths highly ambivalent about the worth of a diploma, desperately desirous of and at the same time discouraged from its achievement. If the process of education is to allow children, adolescents, and adults their voices—to read, write, create, critique, and transform—how can we justify the institutionalizing of silence at a level of policies that obscure systemic problems behind a rhetoric of "excellence" and "progress"; a curriculum bereft of the lived experiences of students themselves; a pedagogy organized around control and not conversation; and a thoroughgoing psychologizing of social issues which enables Patrice to bury herself in silence and not be noticed? A self-critical analysis of the fundamental ways in which we teach children to betray their own voices is crucial.

Sexuality, Schooling, and Adolescent Females: The Missing Discourse of Desire

MICHELLE FINE

Since late 1986, popular magazines and newspapers have printed steamy stories about education and sexuality. Whether the controversy surrounds sex education or school-based health clinics (SBHCs), public discourses of adolescent sexuality are represented forcefully by government officials, New Right spokespersons, educators, "the public," feminists, and healthcare professionals. These stories offer the authority of "facts," insights into the political controversies, and access to unacknowledged fears about sexuality (Foucault, 1980). Although the facts usually involve the adolescent female body, little has been heard from young women themselves.

This chapter examines these diverse perspectives on adolescent sexuality and, in addition, presents the views of a group of adolescent females. The chapter is informed by a study of numerous current sex education curricula, a year of negotiating for inclusion of lesbian and gay sexuality in a citywide sex education curriculum, and interviews and observations gathered in New York City sex education classrooms.[1] The analysis examines the desires, fears, and fantasies which give structure and shape to silences and voices concerning sex education and school-based health clinics in the 1980s.

Chapter 2 previously appeared in *Harvard Educational Review*, 58(1), pp. 29–53, 1988. Used by permission of the *Harvard Educational Review*.

Despite the attention devoted to teen sexuality, pregnancy, and parenting in this country, and despite the evidence of effective interventions and the widespread public support expressed for these interventions (Harris & Associates, 1985), the systematic implementation of sex education and SBHCs continues to be obstructed by the controversies surrounding them (Kantrowitz et al., 1987; Leo, 1986). Those who resist sex education or SBHCs often present their views as based on rationality and a concern for protecting the young. For such opponents, sex education raises questions of promoting promiscuity and immorality, and of undermining family values. Yet the language of the challenges suggests an effect substantially more profound and primitive. Gary Bauer, Undersecretary of Education in the U.S. Department of Education, for example, constructs an image of immorality littered by adolescent sexuality and drug abuse:

> There is ample impressionistic evidence to indicate that drug abuse and promiscuity are not independent behaviors. When inhibitions fall, they collapse across the board. When people of any age lower a sense of right and wrong, the loss is not selective. . . . [T]hey are all expressions of the same ethical vacuum among many teens. . . . (1986)

Even Surgeon General C. Everett Koop, a strong supporter of sex education, recently explained: "[W]e have to be as explicit as necessary. . . . You can't talk of the dangers of snake poisoning and not mention snakes" (quoted in Leo, 1986, p. 54). Such commonly used and often repeated metaphors associate adolescent sexuality with victimization and danger.

Yet public schools have rejected the task of sexual dialogue and critique, or what has been called "sexuality education." Within today's standard sex education curricula and many public school classrooms, we find: (1) the authorized suppression of a discourse of female sexual desire; (2) the promotion of a discourse of female sexual victimization; and (3) the explicit privileging of married heterosexuality over other practices of sexuality. One finds an unacknowledged social ambivalence about female sexuality which ideologically separates the female sexual agent, or subject, from her counterpart, the female sexual victim. The adolescent woman of the 1980s is constructed as the latter. Educated primarily as the potential victim of male sexuality, she represents no subject in her own right. Young women continue to be taught to fear and defend in isolation from exploring desire, and in this context there is little possibility of their developing a critique of gender or sexual arrangements.

PREVAILING DISCOURSES OF FEMALE
SEXUALITY INSIDE PUBLIC SCHOOLS

> If the body is seen as endangered by uncontrollable forces, then presumably this is a society or social group which fears change—change which it perceived simultaneously as powerful and beyond its control. (Smith-Rosenberg, 1978, p. 229)

Public schools have historically been the site for identifying, civilizing, and containing that which is considered uncontrollable. While evidence of sexuality is everywhere within public high schools—in the halls, classrooms, bathrooms, lunchrooms, and the library—official sexuality education occurs sparsely: in social studies, biology, sex education, or inside the nurse's office. To understand how sexuality is managed inside schools, I examined the major discourses of sexuality which characterize the national debates over sex education and SBHCs. These discourses are then tracked as they weave through the curricula, classrooms, and halls of public high schools.

The first discourse, *sexuality as violence*, is clearly the most conservative, and equates adolescent heterosexuality with violence. At the 1986 American Dreams Symposium on education, Phyllis Schlafly commented: "Those courses on sex, abuse, incest, AIDS, they are all designed to terrorize our children. We should fight their existence, and stop putting terror in the hearts and minds of our youngsters." One aspect of this position, shared by women as politically distinct as Schlafly and the radical feminist lawyer Catherine MacKinnon (1983), views heterosexuality as essentially violent and coercive. In its full conservative form, proponents call for the elimination of sex education and clinics and urge complete reliance on the family to dictate appropriate values, mores, and behaviors.

Sexuality as violence presumes that there is a causal relationship between official silence about sexuality and a decrease in sexual activity—therefore, by not teaching about sexuality, adolescent sexual behavior will not occur. The irony, of course, lies in the empirical evidence. Fisher, Byrne, and White (1983) have documented sex-negative attitudes and contraceptive use to be negatively correlated. In their study, sex-negative attitudes do not discourage sexual activity, but they do discourage responsible use of contraception. Teens who believe sexual involvement is wrong deny responsibility for contraception. To accept responsibility would legitimate "bad" behavior. By contrast, Fisher et al. (1983) found that adolescents with sex-positive attitudes tend to be both more consistent and more positive about contraceptive use. By not teaching about sexuality, or by teaching sex-negative attitudes, schools apparently will not forestall sexual activity, but may well discourage responsible contraception.

The second discourse, *sexuality as victimization*, gathers a much greater following. Female adolescent sexuality is represented as a moment of victimization in which the dangers of heterosexuality for adolescent women (and, more recently, of homosexuality for adolescent men) are prominent. While sex may not be depicted as inherently violent, young women (and today, men) learn of their vulnerability to potential male predators.

To avoid being victimized, females learn to defend themselves against disease, pregnancy, and "being used." The discourse of victimization supports sex education, including AIDS education, with parental consent. Suggested classroom activities emphasize "saying no," practicing abstinence, enumerating the social and emotional risks of sexual intimacy, and listing the possible diseases associated with sexual intimacy. The language, as well as the questions asked and not asked, represents females as the actual and potential victims of male desire. In exercises, role plays, and class discussions, girls practice resistance to trite lines, unwanted hands, opened buttons, and the surrender of other "bases" they are not prepared to yield. The discourses of violence and victimization both portray males as potential predators and females as victims. Three problematic assumptions underlie these two views:

- First, female subjectivity, including the desire to engage in sexual activity, is placed outside the prevailing conversation (Vance, 1984).
- Second, both arguments present female victimization as contingent upon unmarried heterosexual involvement—rather than inherent in existing gender, class, and racial arrangements (Ru-

bin, 1984). While feminists have long fought for the legal and social acknowledgment of sexual violence against women, most have resisted the claim that female victimization hinges primarily upon sexual involvement with men. The full range of victimization of women—at work, at home, on the streets—has instead been uncovered. The language and emotion invested in these two discourses divert attention away from structures, arrangements, and relationships which oppress women in general, and low-income women and women of color in particular (Lorde, 1980).

- Third, the messages, while narrowly antisexual, nevertheless buttress traditional heterosexual arrangements. These views assume that as long as females avoid premarital sexual relations with men, victimization can be avoided. Ironically, however, protection from male victimization is available primarily through marriage—by coupling with a man. The paradoxical message teaches females to fear the very men who will ultimately protect them.

The third discourse, *sexuality as individual morality*, introduces explicit notions of sexual subjectivity for women. Although quite judgmental and moralistic, this discourse values women's sexual decision making as long as the decisions made are for premarital abstinence. For example, Secretary of Education William Bennett urges schools to teach "morality literacy" and to educate toward "modesty," "chastity," and "abstinence" until marriage. The language of self-control and self-respect reminds students that sexual immorality breeds not only personal problems but also community tax burdens.

The debate over morality in sex education curricula marks a clear contradiction among educational conservatives over whether and how the state may intervene in the "privacy of families." Noninterventionists, including Schlafly and Onalee McGraw, argue that educators should not teach about sexuality at all. To do so is to take a particular moral position which subverts the family. Interventionists, including Koop, Bennett, and Bauer, argue that schools should teach about sexuality by focusing on "good values," but disagree about how. Koop proposes open discussion of sexuality and the use of condoms, while Bennett advocates "sexual restraint" ("Koop's AIDS Stand Assailed,"

1987). Sexuality in this discourse is posed as a test of self-control; individual restraint triumphs over social temptation. Pleasure and desire for women as sexual subjects remain largely in the shadows, obscured from adolescent eyes.

The fourth discourse, a *discourse of desire,* remains a whisper inside the official work of U.S. public schools. If introduced at all, it is as an interruption of the ongoing conversation (Snitow, Stansell, & Thompson, 1983). The naming of desire, pleasure, or sexual entitlement, particularly for females, barely exists in the formal agenda of public schooling on sexuality. When spoken, it is tagged with reminders of "consequences"—emotional, physical, moral, reproductive, and/or financial (Freudenberg, 1987). A genuine discourse of desire would invite adolescents to explore what feels good and bad, desirable and undesirable, grounded in experiences, needs, and limits. Such a discourse would release females from a position of receptivity, enable an analysis of the dialectics of victimization and pleasure, and would pose female adolescents as subjects of sexuality, initiators as well as negotiators (Petchesky, 1984; Thompson, 1983).

In Sweden, where sex education has been offered in schools since the turn of the century, the State Commission on Sex Education recommends teaching students to "acquire a knowledge . . . [which] will equip them to experience sexual life as a source of happiness and joy in fellowship with other [people]" (Brown, 1983, p. 88). The teachers' handbook goes on, "The many young people who wish to wait [before initiating sexual activity] and those who have had early sexual relations should experience, in class, [the feeling] that they are understood and accepted" (p. 93). Compare this to an exercise suggested in a major U.S. metropolitan sex education curriculum: "Discuss and evaluate: things which may cause teenagers to engage in sexual relations before they are ready to assume the responsibility of marriage" (see Philadelphia School District, 1986; and New York City Board of Education, 1984).

A discourse of desire, though seldom explored in U.S. classrooms, does occur in less structured school situations. The following excerpts, taken from group and individual student interviews, demonstrate female adolescents' subjective experiences of body and desire as they begin to articulate notions of sexuality.

In some cases, young women pose a critique of marriage:

I'm still in love with Simon, but I'm seeing Jose. He's OK but
he said, "Will you be my girl?" I hate that. It feels like they
own you. Like I say to a girlfriend, "What's wrong? You look
terrible!" and she says, "I'm married!" (Millie, a 16-year-old student from the Dominican Republic)

In other cases they offer stories of their own victimization:

It's not like last year. Then I came to school regular. Now my
old boyfriend, he waits for me in front of my building every
morning and he fights with me. Threatens me, gettin' all bad. . . .
I want to move out of my house and live 'cause he ain't gonna
stop no way. (Sylvia, age 17, about to drop out of 12th grade)

Some even speak of desire:

I'm sorry I couldn't call you last night about the interview, but
my boyfriend came back from [the] Navy and I wanted to
spend the night with him, we don't get to see each other much.
(Shandra, age 17, after a no-show for an interview)

In a context in which desire is not silenced, but acknowledged and
discussed, conversations with adolescent women can, as seen here,
educate through a dialectic of victimization and pleasure. Despite formal
silencing, it would be misleading to suggest that talk of desire never
emerges within public schools. Notwithstanding a political climate organized around the suppression of this conversation, some teachers and
community advocates continue to struggle for an empowering sex education curriculum both in and out of the high school classroom.

Family life curricula and/or plans for a school-based health clinic
have been carefully generated in many communities. Yet they continue
to face loud and sometimes violent resistance by religious and community groups, often from outside the district lines (Boffey, 1987;
"Chicago School Clinic," 1986; Dowd, 1986; Perlez, 1986a, 1986b;
Rohter, 1985). In other communities, when curricula or clinics have
been approved with little overt confrontation, monies for training are
withheld. For example, in New York City in 1987, $1.7 million was
initially requested to implement training on the Family Life education
curriculum. As sex educators confronted community and religious

groups, the inclusion of some topics as well as the language of others were continually negotiated. Ultimately, the chancellor requested only $600,000 for training, a sum substantially inadequate to the task.[2]

In this political context many public school educators nevertheless continue to take personal and professional risks to create materials and foster classroom environments which speak fully to the sexual subjectivities of young women and men. Some operate within the privacy of their classrooms, subverting the official curriculum and engaging students in critical discussion. Others advocate publicly for enriched curricula and training. A few have even requested that community-based advocates *not* agitate for official curricular change, so "we [teachers] can continue to do what we do in the classroom, with nobody looking over our shoulders. You make a big public deal of this, and it will blow open."[3] Within public school classrooms, it seems that female desire may indeed be addressed when educators act subversively. But in the typical sex education classroom, silence, and therefore distortion, surrounds female desire.

The blanketing of female sexual subjectivity in public school classrooms, in public discourse, and in bed will sound familiar to those who have read Luce Irigaray (1980) and Helene Cixous (1981). These French feminists have argued that expressions of female voice, body, and sexuality are essentially inaudible when the dominant language and ways of viewing are male. Inside the hegemony of what they call The Law of the Father, female desire and pleasure can gain expression only in the terrain already charted by men (see also Burke, 1980). In the public school arena, this constriction of what is called sexuality allows girls one primary decision—to say yes or no—to a question not necessarily their own. A discourse of desire in which young women have a voice would be informed and generated out of their own socially constructed sexual meanings. It is to these expressions that we now turn.

THE BODIES OF FEMALE ADOLESCENTS: VOICES AND STRUCTURED SILENCES

If four discourses can be distinguished among the many positions articulated by various "authorities," the sexual meanings voiced by female adolescents defy such classification. A discourse of desire, though absent in the "official" curriculum, is by no means missing from the lived experiences or commentaries of young women. This section introduces their sexual thoughts, concerns, and meanings, as represented by a group of Black and Latina female adolescents—students and dropouts from a public high school in New York City serving predominantly low-income youths. In my year at this comprehensive high school I had frequent opportunity to speak with adolescents and listen to them talk about sex. The comments reported derive from conversations between the young women and their teachers, among themselves, and with me, as researcher. During conversations, the young women talked freely about fears and, in the same breath, asked about passions. Their struggle to untangle issues of gender, power, and sexuality underscores the fact that, for them, notions of sexual negotiation cannot be separated from sacrifice and nurturance.

The adolescent female rarely reflects simply on sexuality. Her sense of sexuality is informed by peers, culture, religion, violence, history, passion, authority, rebellion, body, past and future, and gender and racial relations of power (Espin, 1984; Omolade, 1983). The adolescent woman herself assumes a dual consciousness—at once taken with the excitement of actual/anticipated sexuality and consumed with anxiety and worry. While too few safe spaces exist for adolescent women's exploration of sexual subjectivities, there are all too many dangerous spots for their exploitation.

Whether in a classroom, on the street, at work, or at home, the adolescent female's sexuality is negotiated by, for, and despite the young woman herself. Patricia, a young Puerto Rican woman who worried about her younger sister, relates: "You see, I'm the love child and she's the one born because my mother was raped in Puerto Rico. Her father's in jail now, and she feels so bad about the whole thing so she acts bad." For Patricia, as for the many young women who have experienced and/or witnessed sexual violence, discussions of sexuality merge representations of passion with violence. Often the initiator of conversation among peers about virginity, orgasm, "getting off," and pleasure, Patricia mixed sexual talk freely with references to force and violence. She is a poignant narrator who illustrates, from the female adolescent's perspective, that sexual victimization and desire coexist (Benjamin, 1983).

Sharlene and Betty echo this braiding of danger and desire. Sharlene explained: "Boys always be trying to get into my panties," and

Betty added: "I don't be needin' a man who won't give me no pleasure but take my money and expect me to take care of him." This powerful commentary on gender relations, voiced by Black adolescent females, was inseparable from their views of sexuality. To be a woman was to be strong, independent, and reliable—but not too independent for fear of scaring off a man.

Deidre continued this conversation, explicitly pitting male fragility against female strength: "Boys in my neighborhood ain't wrapped so tight. Got to be careful how you treat them. . . . " She reluctantly admitted that perhaps it is more important for Black males than females to attend college, "Girls and women, we're stronger, we take care of ourselves. But boys and men, if they don't get away from the neighborhood, they end up in jail, on drugs or dead . . . or wack [crazy]."

These young women spoke often of anger at males, while concurrently expressing a strong desire for mate attention: "I dropped out 'cause I fell in love, and couldn't stop thinking of him." An equally compelling desire was to protect young males—particularly Black males—from a system which "makes them wack." Ever aware of the ways that institutional racism and the economy have affected Black males, these young women seek pleasure but also offer comfort. They often view self-protection as taking something away from young men. Lavanda offered a telling example: "If I ask him to use a condom, he won't feel like a man."

In order to understand the sexual subjectivities of young women more completely, educators need to reconstruct schooling as an empowering context in which we listen to and work with the meanings and experiences of gender and sexuality revealed by the adolescents themselves. When we refuse that responsibility, we prohibit an education which adolescents wholly need and deserve. My classroom observations suggest that such education is rare.

Ms. Rosen, a teacher of a sex education class, opened one session with a request: "You should talk to your mother or father about sex before you get involved." Nilda initiated what became an informal protest by a number of Latino students: "Not our parents! We tell them one little thing and they get crazy. My cousin got sent to Puerto Rico to live with her religious aunt, and my sister got beat 'cause my father thought she was with a boy." For these adolescents, a safe space for discussion, critique, and construction of sexualities was not something they found in their homes. Instead, they relied on school, the spot they chose for the safe exploration of sexualities.

The absence of safe spaces for exploring sexuality affects all adolescents. It was paradoxical to realize that perhaps the only students who had an in-school opportunity for critical sexual discussion in the comfort of peers were the few students who had organized the Gay and Lesbian Association (GALA) at the high school. While most lesbian, gay, or bisexual students were undoubtedly closeted, those few who were "out" claimed this public space for their display and for their sanctuary. Exchanging support when families and peers would offer little, GALA members worried that so few students were willing to come out, and that so many suffered the assaults of homophobia individually. The gay and lesbian rights movement had powerfully affected these youngsters, who were comfortable enough to support each other in a place not considered very safe—a public high school in which echoes of "faggot!" fill the halls.

In the absence of an education which explores and unearths danger and desire, sexuality education classes typically provide little opportunity for discussions beyond those constructed around superficial notions of male heterosexuality (see Kelly, 1986, for a counterexample). Male pleasure is taught, albeit as biology. Teens learn about "wet dreams" (as the onset of puberty for males), "erection" (as the preface to intercourse), and "ejaculation" (as the act of inseminating). Female pleasures and questions are far less often the topic of discussion. Few voices of female sexual agency can be heard. The language of victimization and its underlying concerns—"Say No," put a brake on his sexuality, don't encourage—ultimately deny young women the right to control their own sexuality by providing no access to a legitimate position of sexual subjectivity. Often conflicted about self-representation, adolescent females spend enormous amounts of time trying to "save it," "lose it," convince others that they have lost or saved it, or trying to be "discreet" instead of focusing their energies in ways that are sexually autonomous, responsible, and pleasurable. In classroom observations, girls who were heterosexually active rarely spoke, for fear of being ostracized (Fine, 1986). Those who were heterosexual virgins had the same worry. And most students who were gay, bisexual, or lesbian remained closeted, aware of the very real dangers of homophobia.

Occasionally, the difficult and pleasurable aspects of sexuality were discussed together, coming either as an interruption, or because an educational context was constructed. During a social studies class, for example, Catherine, the proud mother of 2-year-old Tiffany, challenged an assumption underlying the class discussion—that teen motherhood devastates mother and child; "If I didn't get pregnant I would have continued on a downward path, going nowhere. They say teenage pregnancy is bad for you, but it was good for me. I know I can't mess around now, I got to worry about what's good for Tiffany and for me."

Another interruption came from Opal, a young Black student. Excerpts from her hygiene class follow.

October 23: Hygiene Class

Teacher: Let's talk about teenage pregnancy.

Opal: How come girls in the locker room say, "You a virgin?" and if you say "Yeah" they laugh and say "Ohh, you're a virgin. . . . " And some Black teenagers, I don't mean to be racial, when they get ready to tell their mothers they had sex, some break on them and some look funny. My friend told her mother and she broke all the dishes. She told her mother so she could get protection so she don't get pregnant.

Teacher: When my thirteen-year-old (relative) asked for birth control I was shocked and angry.

Portia: Mothers should help so she can get protection and not get pregnant or diseases. So you was wrong.

Teacher: Why not say "I'm thinking about having sex?"

Portia: You tell them after, not before, having sex but before pregnancy.

Teacher (now angry): Then it's a fait accompli and you expect my compassion? You have to take more responsibility.

Portia: I am! If you get pregnant after you told your mother and you got all the stuff and still get pregnant, you the fool. Take up hygiene and learn. Then it's my responsibility if I end up pregnant. . . .

Two days later, the discussion continued.

October 25: Hygiene Class

Teacher: What topics should we talk about in sex education?

Portia: Organs, how they work.

Opal: What's an orgasm?

[laughter]

Teacher: Sexual response, sensation all over the body. What's
    analogous to the male penis on the female?

Theo: Clitoris.

Teacher: Right, go home and look in the mirror.

Portia: She is too much!

Teacher: Why look in the mirror?

Elaine: It's yours.

Teacher: Why is it important to know what your body looks
    like?

Opal: You should like your body.

Teacher: You should know what it looks like when it's healthy,
    so you can recognize problems like vaginal warts.

The discourse of desire, initiated by Opal but evident only as an interruption, faded rapidly into the discourse of disease—warning about the dangers of sexuality.

It was in the spring of that year that Opal showed up pregnant. Her hygiene teacher, who was extremely concerned and involved with her students, was also quite angry with Opal: "Who is going to take care of that baby, you or your mother? You know what it costs to buy diapers and milk and afford child care?"

Opal, in conversation with me, related, "I got to leave [school] 'cause even if they don't say it, them teachers got hate in their eyes when they look at my belly." In the absence of a way to talk about passion, pleasure, danger, and responsibility, this teacher fetishized the latter two, holding the former two hostage. Because adolescent females combine these experiences in their daily lives, the separation is false, judgmental, and ultimately not very educational.

Over the year in this high school, and in other public schools since, I have observed a systematic refusal to name issues, particularly issues that caused adults discomfort. Educators often projected their discomfort onto students in the guise of "protecting" them (Fine, 1987). An example of such silencing can be seen in a (now altered) policy of the school district of Philadelphia. In 1985 a student informed me, "We're not allowed to talk about abortion in our school." Assuming this was an overstatement, I asked an administrator at the district about this practice. She explained, "That's not quite right. If a student asks a question about abortion, the teacher can define abortion, she just can't discuss it." How can definition occur without discussion, exchange, conversation, or critique unless a subtext of silencing prevails (Greene, 1986; Noddings, 1986)?

Explicit silencing of abortion has since been lifted in Philadelphia. The revised curriculum now reads:

Options for unintended pregnancy:
> (a) adoption
> (b) foster care
> (c) single parenthood
> (d) teen marriage
> (e) abortion

A footnote is supposed to be added, however, to elaborate the negative consequences of abortion. In the social politics that surround public schools, such compromises are apparent across cities.

The New York City Family Life Education curriculum reads similarly (New York City Board of Education, 1984, p. 172):

List: The possible options for an unintended pregnancy. What considerations should be given in the decision on the alternatives?

- adoption
- foster care
- mother keeps baby
- elective abortion

Discuss:

- religious viewpoints on abortion
- present laws concerning abortion
- current developments in prenatal diagnosis and their implication for abortion issues
- why abortion should not be considered a contraceptive device

List: The people or community services that could provide assistance in the event of an unintended pregnancy.
Invite: A speaker to discuss alternatives to abortion; for example, a social worker from the Department of Social Services to discuss foster care.

One must be suspicious when diverse views are sought only for abortion, and not for adoption, teen motherhood, or foster care. The call to silence is easily identified in current political and educational contexts (Fine, 1987; Foucault, 1980). The silence surrounding contraception and abortion options and diversity in sexual orientations denies adolescents information and sends the message that such conversations are taboo—at home, at church, and even at school.

In contrast to these "official curricula," which allow discussion and admission of desire only as an interruption, let us examine other situations in which young women were invited to analyze sexuality across categories of the body, the mind, the heart, and, of course, gender politics.

Teen Choice, a voluntary counseling program in New York City, held on-site by nonboard of education social workers, offered an instance in which the complexities of pleasure and danger were invited, analyzed, and braided into discussions of sexuality. In a small group discussion, the counselor asked of the 7 ninth graders, "What are the two functions of a penis?" One student responded, "To pee!" Another student offered the second function: "To eat!" which was followed by laughter and serious discussion. The conversation proceeded as the teacher asked, "Do all penises look alike?" The students explained, "No, they are all different colors!"

The freedom to express, beyond simple right and wrong answers, enabled these young women to offer what they knew with humor and delight. This discussion ended as one student insisted that if you "jump up and down a lot, the stuff will fall out of you and you won't get pregnant," to which the social worker answered with slight exasperation that millions of sperm would have to be released for such "expulsion" to work, and that of course, it wouldn't work. In this conversation one could hear what seemed like too much experience, too little information, and too few questions asked by the students. But the discussion, which was sex-segregated and guided by the experiences and questions of the students themselves (and the skills of the social worker), enabled easy movement between pleasure and danger, safety and desire, naiveté and knowledge, and victimization and entitlement.

What is evident, then, is that even in the absence of a discourse of desire, young women express their notions of sexuality and relate their experiences. Yet, "official" discourses of sexuality leave little room for such exploration. The authorized sexual discourses define what is safe, what is taboo, and what will be silenced. This discourse of sexuality miseducates adolescent women. What results is a discourse of sexuality based on the male in search of desire and the female in search of protection. The open, coed sexuality discussions so many fought for in the 1970s have been appropriated as a forum for the primacy of male heterosexuality and the preservation of female victimization.

THE POLITICS OF FEMALE SEXUAL SUBJECTIVITIES

In 1912, an education committee explicitly argued that "scientific" sex education "should . . . keep sex consciousness and sex emotions at the minimum" (Leo, 1986). In the same era G. Stanley Hall proposed diversionary pursuits for adolescents, including hunting, music, and sports, "to reduce sex stress and tension . . . to short-circuit, transmute it and turn it on to develop the higher powers of the men [sic]" (Hall, 1914, pp. 29, 30). In 1915 Orison Marden, author of *The Crime of Silence*, chastised educators, reformers, and public health specialists for their unwillingness to speak publicly about sexuality and for relying inappropriately on parents and peers, who were deemed too ignorant to provide sex instruction (Imber, 1984; Strong, 1972). And in 1921, radical sex educator Maurice Bigelow wrote:

> Now, most scientifically-trained women seem to agree that there are no corresponding phenomena in the early pubertal life of the normal young woman who has good health (corresponding to male masturbation). A limited number of mature women, some of them physicians, report having experienced in the pubertal years localized tumescence and other disturbances which made them definitely conscious of sexual instincts. However, it should be noted that most of these are known to have had a personal history including one or more such abnormalities such as dysmenorrhea, uterine displacement, pathological ovaries, leucorrhea, tuberculosis, masturbation, neurasthenia, nymphomania, or other disturbances which are sufficient to account for local sexual stimulation. In short such women are not normal. . . . (p. 179)

In the 1950s, public school health classes separated girls from boys. Girls "learned about sex" by watching films of the accelerated development of breasts and hips, the flow of menstrual blood, and then the progression of venereal disease as a result of participation in out-of-wedlock heterosexual activity.

Thirty years and a much-debated sexual revolution later (Ehren-reich, Hess, & Jacobs, 1986), much has changed. Feminism, the Civil Rights Movement, the disability and gay rights movements, birth control, legal abortion with federal funding (won and then lost), and reproductive technologies are part of these changes (Weeks, 1985). Due both to the consequences of, and the backlashes against, these movements, students today do learn about sexuality—if typically through the representations of female sexuality as inadequacy or vic-timization, male homosexuality as a story of predator and prey, and male heterosexuality as desire.

Young women today know that female sexual subjectivity is at least not an inherent contradiction. Perhaps they even feel it is an entitlement. Yet when public schools resist acknowledging the fullness of female sexual subjectivities, they reproduce a profound social am-bivalence which dichotomizes female heterosexuality (Espin, 1984; Omolade, 1983). This ambivalence surrounds a fragile cultural distinc-tion between two forms of female sexuality: *consensual* sexuality, repre-senting consent or choice in sexuality, and *coercive* sexuality, which represents force, victimization, and/or crime (Weeks, 1985).

During the 1980s, however, this distinction began to be challenged. It was acknowledged that gender-based power inequities shape, de-fine, and construct experiences of sexuality. Notions of sexual consent and force, except in extreme circumstances, became complicated, no longer in simple opposition. The first problem concerned how to con-ceptualize power asymmetries and consensual sexuality. Could *consen-sual* female heterosexuality be said to exist within a context replete with structures, relationships, acts, and threats of female victimization (sexual, social, and economic) (MacKinnon, 1983)? How could we speak of "sexual preference" when sexual involvement outside of heterosex-uality may seriously jeopardize one's social and/or economic well-being (Petchesky, 1984)? Diverse female sexual subjectivities emerge through, despite, and because of gender-based power asymmetries. To imagine a female sexual self, free of and uncontaminated by power, was rendered naive (Foucault, 1980; Irigaray, 1980; Rubin, 1984).

The second problem involved the internal incoherence of the cate-gories. Once assumed fully independent, the two began to blur as the varied practices of sexuality went public. At the intersection of these presumably parallel forms—coercive and consensual sexualities—lay "sexual" acts of violence and "violent" acts of sex. "Sexual" acts of violence, including marital rape, acquaintance rape, and sexual harassment, were historically considered consensual. A woman involved in a marriage, on a date, or working outside her home "naturally" risked receiving sexual attention; her consent was inferred from her presence. But today, in many states, this woman can sue her husband for such sexual acts of violence; in all states, she can prosecute a boss. What was once part of "domestic life" or "work" may, today, be criminal. On the other hand, "violent" acts of sex, including consensual sadomasochism and the use of violence-portraying pornography, were once considered inherently coercive for women (Benjamin, 1983; Rubin, 1984; Weeks, 1985). Female involvement in such sexual practices historically had been dismissed as nonconsensual. Today such romanticizing of a naive and moral "feminine sexuality" has been challenged as essentialist, and the assumption that such a feminine sexuality is "natural" to women has been shown to be false (Rubin, 1984).

Over the past decade, understandings of female sexual choice, consent, and coercion have grown richer and more complex. While questions about female subjectivities have become more interesting, the answers (for some) remain deceptively simple. Inside public schools, for example, female adolescents continue to be educated as though they were the potential *victims* of sexual (male) desire. By contrast, the ideological opposition represents only adult married women as fully consensual partners. The distinction of coercion and consent has been organized simply and respectively around age and marital status—which effectively resolves any complexity and/or ambivalence.

The ambivalence surrounding female heterosexuality places the victim and subject in opposition and derogates all women who represent female sexual subjectivities outside of marriage—prostitutes, lesbians, single mothers, women involved with multiple partners, and particularly, Black single mothers (Weitz, 1984). "Protected" from this derogation, the typical adolescent woman, as represented in sex education curricula, is without any sexual subjectivity. The discourse of victimization not only obscures the derogation, it also transforms socially distributed anxieties about female sexuality into acceptable, and even protective, talk.

The fact that schools implicitly organize sex education around a concern for female victimization is suspect, however, for two reasons.

First, if female victims of male violence were truly a social concern, wouldn't the victims of rape, incest, and sexual harassment encounter social compassion, and not suspicion and blame? And second, if sex education were designed primarily to prevent victimization but not to prevent exploration of desire, wouldn't there be more discussions of both the pleasures and relatively fewer risks of disease or pregnancy associated with lesbian relationships and protected sexual intercourse, or of the risk-free pleasures of masturbation and fantasy? Public education's concern for the female victim is revealed as deceptively thin when real victims are discredited, and when nonvictimizing pleasures are silenced.

This unacknowledged social ambivalence about heterosexuality polarizes the debates over sex education and school-based health clinics. The anxiety effectively treats the female sexual victim as though she were a completely separate species from the female sexual subject. Yet the adolescent women quoted earlier in this text remind us that the female victim and subject coexist in every woman's body.

TOWARD A DISCOURSE OF SEXUAL DESIRE AND SOCIAL ENTITLEMENT: IN THE STUDENT BODIES OF PUBLIC SCHOOLS

I have argued that silencing a discourse of desire buttresses the icon of woman-as-victim. In so doing, public schooling may actually disable young women in their negotiations as sexual subjects. Trained through and into positions of passivity and victimization, young women are currently educated away from positions of sexual self-interest.

If we re-situate the adolescent woman in a rich and empowering educational context, she develops a sense of self which is sexual as well as intellectual, social, and economic. In this section I invite readers to imagine such a context. The dialectic of desire and victimization—across spheres of labor, social relations, and sexuality—would then frame schooling. While many of the curricula and interventions discussed in this paper are imperfect, data on the effectiveness of what *is* available are nevertheless compelling. Studies of sex education curricula, SBHCs, classroom discussions, and ethnographies of life inside public high schools demonstrate that a sense of sexual and social entitlement for young women *can* be fostered within public schools.

SEX EDUCATION AS INTELLECTUAL EMPOWERMENT

Harris and Yankelovich polls confirm that over 80% of American adults believe that students should be educated about sexuality within their public schools. Seventy-five percent believe that homosexuality and abortion should be included in the curriculum, with 40% of those surveyed by Yankelovich et al. ($N = 1015$) agreeing that 12-year-olds should be taught about oral and anal sex (see Leo, 1986; Harris & Associates, 1985).

While the public continues to debate the precise content of sex education, most parents approve and support sex education for their children. An Illinois program monitored parental requests to "opt out" and found that only 6 or 7 of 850 children were actually excused from sex education courses (Leo, 1986). In a California assessment, fewer than 2% of parents disallowed their children's participation. And in a longitudinal 5-year program in Connecticut, 7 of 2,500 students requested exemption from these classes (Scales, 1981). Resistance to sex education, while loud at the level of public rhetoric and conservative organizing, is both less vocal and less active within schools and parents' groups (Hottois & Milner, 1975; Scales, 1981).

Sex education courses are offered broadly, if not comprehensively, across the United States. In 1981, only 7 of 50 states actually had laws against such instruction, and only one state enforced a prohibition (Kirby & Scales, 1981). Surveying 179 urban school districts, Sonnenstein and Pittman (1984) found that 75% offered some sex education within senior and junior high schools, while 66% of the elementary schools offered sex education units. Most instruction was, however, limited to 10 hours or less, with content focused on anatomy. In his extensive review of sex education programs, Kirby (1985) concludes that less than 10% of all public school students are exposed to what might be considered comprehensive sex education courses.

The progress on AIDS education is more encouraging, and more complex (see Freudenberg, 1987), but cannot be adequately reviewed in this article. It is important to note, however, that a December 1986 report released by the U.S. Conference of Mayors documents that 54% of the 73 largest school districts and 25 state school agencies offer some form of AIDS education (Benedetto, 1987). Today, debates among federal officials—including Secretary of Education Bennett and Surgeon General Koop—and among educators question *when* and *what* to offer in AIDS education. The question is no longer *whether* such education should be promoted.

Not only has sex education been accepted as a function of public schooling, but it has survived empirical tests of effectiveness. Evaluation data demonstrate that sex education can increase contraceptive knowledge and use (Kirby, 1985; Public/Private Ventures, 1987). In terms of sexual activity (measured narrowly in terms of the onset or frequency of heterosexual intercourse), the evidence suggests that sex education does not instigate an earlier onset or increase of such sexual activity (Zelnick & Kim, 1982) and may, in fact, postpone the onset of heterosexual intercourse (Zabin, Hirsch, Smith, Streett, & Hardy, 1986). The data for pregnancy rates appear to demonstrate no effect for exposure to sex education alone (see Dawson, 1986; Kirby, 1985; Marsiglio & Mott, 1986).

Sex education as constituted in these studies is not sufficient to diminish teen pregnancy rates. In all likelihood it would be naive to expect that sex education (especially if only 10 hours in duration) would carry such a "long arm" of effectiveness. While the widespread problem of teen pregnancy must be attributed broadly to economic and social inequities (Jones et al., 1985), sex education remains necessary and sufficient to educate, demystify, and improve contraceptive knowledge and use. In conjunction with material opportunities for enhanced life options, it is believed that sex education and access to contraceptives and abortion can help to reduce the rate of unintended pregnancy among teens (Dryfoos, 1985a, 1985b; National Research Council, 1987).

SCHOOL-BASED HEALTH CLINICS: SEXUAL EMPOWERMENT

The public opinion and effectiveness data for school-based health clinics are even more compelling than those for sex education. Thirty SBHCs provide on-site healthcare services to senior, and sometimes junior, high school students in more than 18 U.S. communities, with an additional 25 communities developing similar programs (Kirby, 1985). These clinics offer, at a minimum, health counseling, referrals, and follow-up examinations. Over 70% conduct pelvic examinations (Kirby, 1985), approximately 52% prescribe contraceptives, and 28%

dispense contraceptives (Leo, 1986). None performs abortions, and few refer for abortions.

All SBHCs require some form of general parental notification and/or consent, and some charge a nominal fee for generic health services. Relative to private physicians, school-based health clinics and other family planning agencies are substantially more willing to provide contraceptive services to unmarried minors without specific parental consent (consent in this case referring explicitly to contraception). Only 1% of national Planned Parenthood affiliates require consent or notification, compared to 10% of public health department programs and 19% of hospitals (Torres & Forrest, 1985).

The consequences of consent provisions for abortion are substantial. Data from two states, Massachusetts and Minnesota, demonstrate that parental consent laws result in increased teenage pregnancies or increased numbers of out-of-state abortions. The Reproductive Freedom Project of the American Civil Liberties Union, in a report which examines the consequences of such consent provisions, details the impact of these statutes on teens, on their familial relationships, and ultimately, on their unwanted children (Reproductive Freedom Project, 1986). In an analysis of the impact of Minnesota's mandatory parental notification law from 1981 to 1985, this report documents over 7,000 pregnancies in teens aged 13–17, 3,500 of whom "went to state court to seek the right to confidential abortions, all at considerable personal cost." The report also notes that many of the pregnant teens did not petition the court, "although their entitlement and need for confidential abortions was as strong or more so than the teenagers who made it to court. . . . Only those minors who are old enough and wealthy enough or resourceful enough are actually able to use the court bypass option" (Reproductive Freedom Project, p. 4).

These consent provisions, with allowance for court bypass, not only increase the number of unwanted teenage pregnancies carried to term, but also extend the length of time required to secure an abortion, potentially endangering the life of the teenage woman, and increasing the costs of the abortion. The provisions may also jeopardize the physical and emotional well-being of some young women and their mothers, particularly when paternal consent is required and the pregnant teenager resides with a single mother. Finally, the consent provisions create a class-based healthcare system. Adolescents able to afford travel to a nearby state, or able to pay a private physician for a confidential abortion, have access to an abortion. Those unable to afford the travel, or those who are unable to contact a private physician, are likely to become teenage mothers (Reproductive Freedom Project, 1986).

In Minneapolis, during the time from 1980 to 1984 when the law was implemented, the birth rate for 15- to 17-year-olds increased 38.4%, while the birth rate for 18- and 19-year-olds—not affected by the law— rose only .3% (Reproductive Freedom Project, 1986). The State of Massachusetts passed a parental consent law which took effect in 1981. An analysis of the impact of that law concludes that "the major impact of the Massachusetts parental consent law has been to send a monthly average of between 90 and 95 of the state's minors across state lines in search of an abortion. This number represents about one in every three minor abortion patients living in Massachusetts" (Cartoof & Klerman, 1986). These researchers, among others, write that parental consent laws could have more devastating effects in larger states, from which access to neighboring states would be more difficult.

The inequalities inherent in consent provisions and the dramatic consequences which result for young women are well recognized. For example, 29 states and the District of Columbia now explicitly authorize minors to grant their own consent for receipt of contraceptive information and/or services, independent of parental knowledge or consent (see Melton & Russo, 1987, for full discussion, and National Research Council, 1987; for a full analysis of the legal, emotional, and physical health problems attendant upon parental consent laws for abortion, see the Reproductive Freedom Project report). More recently, consent laws for abortion in Pennsylvania and California have been challenged as unconstitutional.

Public approval of SBHCs has been slow but consistent. In the 1986 Yankelovich survey, 84% of surveyed adults agree that these clinics should provide birth control information; 36% endorse dispensing of contraceptives to students (Leo, 1986). In 1985, Harris found that 67% of all respondents, including 76% of Blacks and 76% of Hispanics, agree that public schools should establish formal ties with family planning clinics for teens to learn about and obtain contraception (Harris & Associates, 1985). Mirroring the views of the general public, a national sample of school administrators polled by the Education Research Group indicated that more than 50% believe birth control should be offered in school-based clinics; 30% agree that parental permission should be sought, and 27% agree that contraceptives should be dispensed, even if parental consent is not forthcoming. The discouraging news is that 96% of these respondents indicate that their districts do not presently offer such services (Benedetto, 1987; Werner, 1987).

Research on the effectiveness of SBHCs is consistently persuasive. The 3-year Johns Hopkins study of school-based health clinics (Zabin et al., 1986) found that schools in which SBHCs made referrals and dispensed contraceptives noted an increase in the percentage of "virgin" females visiting the program as well as an increase in contraceptive use. They also found a significant reduction in pregnancy rates: There was a 13% increase at experimental schools after 10 months, versus a 50% increase at control schools; after 28 months, pregnancy rates decreased 30% at experimental schools versus a 53% increase at control schools. Furthermore, by the second year, a substantial percentage of males visited the clinic (48% of males in experimental schools indicated that they "have ever been to a birth control clinic or to a physician about birth control," compared to 12% of males in control schools). Contrary to common belief, the schools in which clinics dispensed contraceptives showed a substantial postponement of first experience of heterosexual intercourse among high school students and an increase in the proportion of young women visiting the clinic prior to "first coitus."

Paralleling the Hopkins findings, the St. Paul Maternity and Infant Care Project (1985, pp. 46–47) found that pregnancy rates dropped substantially in schools with clinics, from 79 births/1,000 (1973) to 26 births/1,000 (1984). Teens who delivered and kept their infants had an 80% graduation rate, relative to approximately 50% of young mothers nationally. Those who stayed in school reported a 1.3% repeat birth rate, compared to 17% nationally. Over 3 years, pregnancy rates dropped by 40%. Twenty-five percent of young women in the school received some form of family planning and 87% of clients were continuing to use contraception at a 3-year follow-up. There were fewer obstetric complications; fewer babies were born at low birth weights; and prenatal visits to physicians increased relative to students in the control schools.

Predictions that school-based health clinics would advance the onset of sexual intimacy, heighten the degree of "promiscuity" and incidence of pregnancy, and hold females primarily responsible for sexuality were countered by the evidence. The onset of sexual intimacy was postponed, while contraception was used more reliably. Pregnancy rates substantially diminished and, over time, a large group of males began to view contraception as a shared responsibility.

It is worth restating here that females who received family planning counseling and/or contraception actually postponed the onset of heterosexual intercourse. I would argue that the availability of such services may enable females to feel they are sexual agents, entitled and therefore responsible, rather than at the constant and terrifying mercy of a young man's pressure to "give in" or of a parent's demands to "save yourself." With a sense of sexual agency and not necessarily urgency, teen girls may be less likely to use or be used by pregnancy (Petchesky, 1984).

NONTRADITIONAL VOCATIONAL TRAINING: SOCIAL AND ECONOMIC ENTITLEMENT

The literature reviewed suggests that sex education, access to contraception, and opportunities for enhanced life options, in combination (Dryfoos, 1985a, 1985b; Kirby, 1985), can significantly diminish the likelihood that a teenager will become pregnant, carry to term, and/ or have a repeat pregnancy, and can increase the likelihood that she will stay in high school through graduation (National Research Council, 1987). Education toward entitlement—including a sense of sexual, economic, and social entitlement—may be sufficient to affect adolescent girls' views on sexuality, contraception, and abortion. By framing female subjectivity within the context of social entitlement, sex education would be organized around dialogue and critique, SBHCs would offer health services, options counseling, contraception, and abortion referrals, and the provision of real "life options" would include nontraditional vocational training programs and employment opportunities for adolescent females (Dryfoos, 1985a, 1985b).

In a nontraditional vocational training program in New York City designed for young women, many of whom are mothers, participants' attitudes toward contraception and abortion shifted once they acquired a set of vocational skills, a sense of social entitlement, and a sense of personal competence (Weinbaum, personal communication, 1986). The young women often began the program without strong academic skills or a sense of competence. At the start, they were more likely to express more negative sentiments about contraception and abortion than when they completed the program. One young woman, who initially held strong antiabortion attitudes, learned that she was pregnant midway through her carpentry apprenticeship. She decided to abort, reasoning that now that she has a future, she can't risk losing it for another baby (Weinbaum, paraphrase of personal communication, 1986). A developing sense of social entitlement may have transformed this young woman's view of reproduction, sexuality, and self.

The Manpower Development Research Corporation (MDRC), in its evaluation of Project Redirection (Polit, Kahn, & Stevens, 1985) offers similar conclusions about a comprehensive vocational training and community-based mentor project for teen mothers and mothers-to-be. Low-income teens were enrolled in Project Redirection, a network of services designed to instill self-sufficiency, in which community women served as mentors. The program included training for what is called "employability," Individual Participation Plans, and peer group sessions. Data on education, employment, and pregnancy outcomes were collected at 12 and 24 months after enrollment. Two years after the program began, many newspapers headlined the program as a failure. The data actually indicated that at 12 months, the end of program involvement, Project Redirection women were significantly *less likely* to experience a repeat pregnancy than comparison women; *more likely* to be using contraception; *more likely* to be in school, to have completed school, or to be in the labor force; and twice as likely (20% versus 11%, respectively) to have earned a Graduate Equivalency Diploma. At 24 months, however, approximately one year out of the program, Project and comparison women were virtually indistinguishable. MDRC reported equivalent rates of repeat pregnancies, dropout, and unemployment.

The Project Redirection data demonstrate that sustained outcomes cannot be expected once programs have been withdrawn and participants confront the realities of a dismal economy and inadequate child care and social services. The data confirm, however, the effectiveness of comprehensive programs to reduce teen pregnancy rates and encourage study or work as long as the young women are actively engaged. Supply-side interventions—changing people but not structures or opportunities—which leave unchallenged an inhospitable and discriminating economy and a thoroughly impoverished child care/

social welfare system are inherently doomed to long-term failure. When such programs fail, the social reading is that "these young women can't be helped." Blaming the victim obscures the fact that the current economy and social welfare arrangements need overhauling if the sustained educational, social, and psychological gains accrued by the Project Redirection participants are to be maintained.

In the absence of enhanced life options, low-income young women are likely to default to early and repeat motherhood as a source of perceived competence, significance, and pleasure. When life options are available, however, a sense of competence and "entitlement to better" may help to prevent second pregnancies, may help to encourage education and, when available, the pursuit of meaningful work (Burt, Kimmich, Goldmuntz, & Sonnenstein, 1984).

FEMININITY MAY BE HAZARDOUS TO HER HEALTH: THE ABSENCE OF ENTITLEMENT

Growing evidence suggests that women who lack a sense of social or sexual entitlement, who hold traditional notions of what it means to be female—self-sacrificing and relatively passive—and who undervalue themselves, are disproportionately likely to find themselves with an unwanted pregnancy and to maintain it through to motherhood. While many young women who drop out, pregnant or not, are not at all traditional in these ways, but are quite feisty and are fueled with a sense of entitlement (Fine, 1986; Weinbaum, personal communication, 1987), it may also be the case that young women who do internalize such notions of "femininity" are disproportionately at risk for pregnancy and dropping out.

The Hispanic Policy Development Project reports that low-income female sophomores who, in 1980, expected to be married and/or to have a child by age 19 were disproportionately represented among nongraduates in 1984. Expectations of early marriage and childbearing correspond to dramatic increases (200 to 400%) in nongraduation rates for low-income adolescent women across racial and ethnic groups (Hispanic Policy Development Project, 1987). These indicators of traditional notions of womanhood bode poorly for female academic achievement.

The Children's Defense Fund (1986) recently published additional data which demonstrate that young women with poor basic skills are three times more likely to become teen parents than women with average or above-average basic skills. Those with poor or fair basic skills are four times more likely to have more than one child while a teen; 29% of women in the bottom skills quintile became mothers by age 18 versus 5% of young women in the top quintile. While academic skill problems must be placed in the context of alienating and problematic schools, and not viewed as inherent in these young women, those who fall in the bottom quintile may nevertheless be the least likely to feel entitled or in control of their lives. They may feel more vulnerable to male pressure or more willing to have a child as a means of feeling competent.

My own observations, derived from a yearlong ethnographic study of a comprehensive public high school in New York City, further confirm some of these conclusions. Six months into the ethnography, new pregnancies began showing. I noticed that many of the girls who got pregnant and carried to term were not those whose bodies, dress, and manner evoked sensuality and experience. Rather, a number of the pregnant women were those who were quite passive and relatively quiet in their classes. One young woman, who granted me an interview anytime, washed the blackboard for her teacher, rarely spoke in class, and never disobeyed her mother, was pregnant by the spring of the school year (Fine, 1986).

Simple stereotypes, of course, betray the complexity of circumstances under which young women become pregnant and maintain their pregnancies. While U.S. rates of teenage sexual activity and age of "sexual initiation" approximate those of comparable developed countries, the teenage pregnancy, abortion, and childbearing rates in the United States are substantially higher. In the United States, teenagers under age 15 are at least five times more likely to give birth than similarly aged teens in other industrialized nations (Jones et al., 1985; National Research Council, 1987). The national factors which correlate with low teenage birthrates include adolescent access to sex education and contraception, and relative equality in the distribution of wealth. Economic and structural conditions which support a class-stratified society, and which limit adolescent access to sexual information and contraception, contribute to inflated teenage pregnancy rates and birthrates.

This broad national context acknowledged, it might still be argued that within our country, traditional notions of what it means to be a woman—to remain subordinate, dependent, self-sacrificing, compliant, and ready to marry and/or bear children early—do little to empower women or enhance a sense of entitlement. This is not to say that teenage dropouts or mothers tend to be of any one type. Yet it may well be that the traditions and practices of "femininity" as commonly understood may be hazardous to the economic, social, educational, and sexual development of young women.

In summary, the historic silencing within public schools of conversations about sexuality, contraception, and abortion, as well as the absence of a discourse of desire—in the form of comprehensive sex education, school-based health clinics, and viable life options via vocational training and placement—all combine to exacerbate the vulnerability of young women whom schools, and the critics of sex education and SBHCs, claim to protect.

CONCLUSION

Adolescents are entitled to a discussion of desire instead of the antisex rhetoric which controls the controversies around sex education, SBHCs, and AIDS education. The absence of a discourse of desire, combined with the lack of analysis of the language of victimization, may actually retard the development of sexual subjectivity and responsibility in students. Those most "at risk" of victimization through pregnancy, disease, violence, or harassment—all female students, low-income females in particular, and nonheterosexual males—are those most likely to be victimized by the absence of critical conversation in public schools. Public schools can no longer afford to maintain silence around a discourse of desire. This is not to say that the silencing of a discourse of desire is the primary root of sexual victimization, teen motherhood, and the concomitant poverty experienced by young and low-income females. Nor could it be responsibly argued that interventions initiated by public schools could ever be successful if separate from economic and social development. But it is important to understand that by providing education, counseling, contraception, and abortion referrals, as well as meaningful educational and vocational opportunities, public schools could play an essential role in the construction of the female subject—social and sexual.

And by not providing such an educational context, public schools contribute to the rendering of substantially different outcomes for male and female students, and for male and female dropouts (Fine, 1986). The absence of a thorough sex education curriculum, of school-based health clinics, of access to free and confidential contraceptive and abortion services, of exposure to information about the varieties of sexual pleasures and partners, and of involvement in sustained employment training programs may so jeopardize the educational and economic outcomes for female adolescents as to constitute sex discrimination. How can we ethically continue to withhold educational treatments we know to be effective for adolescent women?

Public schools constitute a sphere in which young women could be offered access to a language and experience of empowerment. In such contexts, "well-educated" young women could breathe life into positions of social critique and experience entitlement rather than victimization, autonomy rather than terror.

Constructing the "Other": Discursive Renditions of White Working-Class Males in High School

Lois Weis

A key development in postmodern/poststructuralist and feminist research has been the introduction of issues of silencing and voice into research on schools and schooling (Giroux, 1991; Lather, 1991; McLaren, 1991). We no longer speak of reproduction in terms of relations that sustain and/or challenge the economy, but rather have expanded and challenged these considerations to include issues of voice, power, and privilege, drawing upon the well-known work of Michel Foucault (1990) and others. We speak now of "regimes of truth"—of what is known, not known, practiced and not practiced, because of the very language we employ. Our work has changed greatly since the mid-1970s and is alive with lengthy criticism. For we really do seek to understand both the discourse and practice of those whom we study, as well as our own discourse and practice. For, I agree, we must keep the focus on ourselves as we ravel and unravel the lives and practices of others.

Excellent work has been done on the dynamics of power and privilege that nurture, sustain, and legitimate silencing in schools (Michelson, Smith, & Oliver, 1993; Sapon-Shevin, 1993). But as we

---

Chapter 3 is reprinted by permission from *Critical Theory and Educational Research* (pp. 203–222), by Peter L. McLaren & James M. Giarelli (Eds.), the State University of New York Press. Copyright © 1995 State University of New York. All rights reserved.

look closely at this work, we cannot help but notice that the move to silence is an ironic and often ineffective move of power. For within the very centers of structured silence can be heard the most critical and powerful, if excluded, voices of teachers and students in public education. Our move to understand both these practices of silence and how such practices and policies are reworked by real people as they move through educational institutions and our lives must be central to a vital research agenda. All the while, of course, we must continually interrogate ourselves, as authors in this volume and elsewhere do so well (hooks, 1990; McLaren, 1991).

Michelle Fine and I (Weis & Fine, 1993) have recently argued that it is important to acknowledge not only policies and practices that silence, but also those that listen closely to the words, dreams, fantasies, and critiques of those who have dwelt historically at the margins. We must listen closely to the "discursive underground"—to the "political critics" who have little access to the centers of power and privilege. These discursive undergrounds flourish at the margins of our schools. We must reach up from the depths of our own academic language and hear their voices, encourage their centering, if we are sincere about our commitment to a democratic public sphere.

When we listen, we learn many things, not all of which we may find appealing. I want, at this point, to invite you into the text that I created from my work in a steel town, a town hard hit by deindustrialization and a restructured U.S. economy. Arguably the most extreme case of "silencing" in this volume, here I wish to focus on how young White working-class males created "other" at the site of the school. For they did construct the "other" in some very powerful ways, ways that encouraged their own dominance in racial and gendered terms. This setting up as dominant gave most of them permission to roam through vast cultural space and essentially "do nothing." For the young White men simply hung out—they, unlike the young women, had few goals, little direction, virtually no sense of possibility. Their energy went largely into constructing the "other"—the Black male and female, the White female. In constructing the "other," they were able to distance themselves from this "other," asserting themselves as superior, as fundamentally unlike that which they constructed as abhorrent and/or in need of protection. I do not mean to imply here that these discourses and practices were created without reference to the world outside the peer group. Obviously this is not the case, and these young men drew upon historical and current discourses and practices about ethnic/racial minorities and women in general. How these discourses and practices became their own, in a sense, is important, however, and I contend that the process of "othering" is an active one. At this point I invite you into the text.

FREEWAY

The data presented here were gathered as part of a large ethnographic study of Freeway High School. I spent the academic year 1985–86 in the high school, acing as a participant-observer for 3 days a week for the entire year. Data were gathered in classrooms, study halls, the cafeteria, extracurricular activities, and through in-depth interviews with over 60 juniors, virtually all teachers of juniors, the vice principals, social workers, guidance counselors, and others. Data collection centered on the junior class, since this is a key point of decision when PSATs, SATs, and so forth must be considered.[1] In addition, this is, in the state where Freeway is located, the time when the bulk of a series of state tests must be taken if entrance to a 4-year college is being considered.[2]

Freeway embodies trends in the U.S. economy. Occupational data for the Standard Metropolitan Statistical Area for 1960–1980 (the latest year for which data are available) suggest that the most striking decreases in the area are found in the categories of "Precision, Craft, and Repair" and "Operators, Fabricators, and Laborers." These two categories constitute virtually all the so-called blue-collar jobs. When combined, data suggest a relative decline of 22.3% in the blue-collar category from 1960 to 1980. A look at some of the more detailed subcategories reveals a more striking decline. Manufacturers, for example, have experienced an overall decline in the area of 35% between 1958 and 1982.

Data also suggest an increase in the "Technical, Sales and Administrative Support" category. These occupations constituted 22.8% of the total in 1960 as compared with close to 31% in 1980, representing an increase of over one third. Increases in "Service" and "Managerial and Professional Specialty" categories also reflect a shift away from industry and toward the availability of service occupations.

The change in the distribution of occupations by gender needs to be clarified here as well. During this same time period, female employment increased 55%, while employment for men decreased 6%. For most occupations in the area, a net increase in employment during this period may be attributed mainly to the increase in employed women and a net decrease to a decrease in employed men.

Although the emerging economy has absorbed women at a faster rate than men, the proportion of full-time female workers is still lower than that of full-time male workers. Thus, 67% of male workers are full time in 1980 as compared with only 43% of females. In addition, full-time female workers earned 56% of what full-time male workers earned in 1980, and women in sales have average incomes that are only 46% of the average income for men. This is particularly important given that a growing number of positions in the Standard Metropolitan Statistical Area are in Sales, and that these are filled disproportionately by women. Such trends are reflective of trends nationwide. A restructured economy has meant that a higher proportion of females is employed in the labor force relative to earlier years, but that females increasingly earn relatively lower wages than males.

In the Freeway area, deindustrialization is exceptionally visible due to the closing of Freeway Steel. The plant payroll in 1960 was at a record high of 168 million, topping 1968 by 14 million. The daily employment was 18,500.

In the first 7 months of 1971, layoffs at the plant numbered 4,000, and decline continued into the 1980s. From 18,500 jobs in 1979, there were only 3,700 production and 600 supervisory workers left in 1983. At the end of 1983, the plant closed.

The larger ethnography was aimed at unraveling the construction of identities of young White males and females in high school, given the radically restructured economy. What became evident, however, was that these identities, particularly in the case of the young White men, were *absolutely contingent* upon the co-construction of Black men and Black women, and White women. These co-constructions became a means of asserting themselves—a means of forming their own identities in crucial and concrete ways. Their own heterosexuality, masculinity, and Whiteness became their assertions in the face of what they had constructed as "other." These discursive constructions were elaborately braided. What I will present here is the story of that "othering."

FREEWAY MALES

One of the most notable aspects of identity among White working-class males is that of sexism. Paul Willis (1977), for example, argues that male White working-class youth identities are formed at least partially in reaction to that of the ideologically constructed identity of females. Mental labor, for example, is not only less valued than manual labor, but it is less valued because it is seen as feminine. This encourages separate spheres for men and women as well as male dominance. The lads also impose upon girlfriends an ideology of domesticity, "the patterns of homely and subcultural capacity and incapacity," all of which stress the restricted role of women (49).

In terms of the affirmation of male supremacy, Freeway males exhibit the same virulent sexism uncovered in previous studies. This is particularly striking in the Freeway case, since young women are weaving an identity which in many ways contradicts that which is woven *for* them by young men (Weis, 1990). Although one or two boys seem to exist outside these boundaries, basically White working-class males affirm a rather virulent form of assumed male superiority, which involves the constructed identity of female not only as "other" but also as distinctly "less than" and, therefore, subject to male control. Discussions with males indicate that the vast majority speak of future wives and families in strikingly male-dominant terms. This is in sharp contradiction with the sentiments of young women.

> *LW*: You say you want more kids than your parents have. How many kids do you want?
>
> *Bob*: Five.
>
> *LW*: Who's going to take care of these kids?
>
> *Bob*: My wife, hopefully. Unless she's working too. . . . If she wants to work, we'd figure something out. Day care center, something like that. I'd prefer if she didn't want to. I'd like to have her at home.
>
> *LW*: Why?
>
> *Bob*: I think it's up to the mother to do it [raise children; take care of the home]. I wouldn't want to have a baby-sitter raising my kids. Like, I think the principles should be taught by the parent, not by some baby-sitter.

*   *   *

LW: How about your life ten years from now; what do you think you'll be doing?

Rob: Probably be married. Couple of kids.

LW: Do you think your wife will work?

Rob: Hopefully she won't have to 'cause I'll make enough money.

LW: Would you rather she didn't work?

Rob: Naw [Yes, I'd rather she didn't work].

LW: Women shouldn't work?

Rob: Housework.

* * *

Jim: Yes, I'd like to get married, like to get myself a nice house, with kids.

LW: Who is going to be taking care of those kids?

Jim: Depends how rich I am. If I'm making a good salary I assume that the wife, if she wanted to, would stay home and tend to the kids. If there was ever a chance when she wanted to go someplace, fine, I'd watch the kids. Nothing wrong with that. Equal responsibility because when you were consummating the marriage it was equal responsibility.

LW: So, you're willing to assume it?

Jim: Up to a certain point. . . . Like if she says I'm going to go out and get a job and you take care of the kids, "You draw all day" [he wants to be a commercial artist]. "So, I draw; that's what's been supporting us for so many years" I mean, if she starts dictating to me . . . there has to be a good discussion about the responsibilities.

When both parents work, it's been proven that the amount of education they learn, it goes down the tubes, or they get involved in drugs. Half the kids who have drug problems, both of their parents work. If they are doing terribly in school, their parents work.

* * *

LW: When you get married, what will your wife be doing?

Lanny: Well, before we had any kids, she'd be working, but if we had kids, she wouldn't work, she'd be staying home, taking care of the kids.

*   *   *

Seth: I wouldn't mind my wife working as far as secretarial work or something like that. Whatever she wanted to do and she pursued as a career. If there was children around, I'd like her to be at home, so I'd like my job to compensate for just me working and my wife being at home.

*   *   *

LW: Do you think your wife would want to work?

Sam: I wouldn't want her to work.

*   *   *

LW: Let's say you did get married and have children, and your wife wanted to work.

Bill: It all depends on if I had a good job. If the financial situation is bad and she had to go to work, she had to go to work.

LW: And if you got a good job?

Bill: She'd probably be a regular woman.

LW: Staying at home? Why is that a good thing?

Bill: I don't know if it's a good thing, but it'd probably be the normal thing.

It is striking in the above that these young men have constructed women as caretakers and themselves as the sole providers. It is particularly key that these young men expect their wives to be home taking care of the children once children are born. In fact, one of the boys brings to bear what he sees as scientific evidence to argue that "It's been proven . . . half the kids who have drug problems, both of their parents work; if they are doing terribly in school, their parents work." They wish to see their own income sufficient to assume sole support of the family. This dominance in the workplace and in the family is set up in relation to women. They have constructed women in a particular light, despite home lives which contradict this and, to some extent at least, competing discursive messages in the wider society about women in the workforce.

Only a handful of boys constructed a future other than that above. Significantly, only one boy constructed a future in which his wife *should* work, although he does not talk about children. A few boys reflect the sentiment that marriage is a "ball and chain" and one boy said the high divorce rate makes marriage less than attractive.

> *LW*: What kind of person do you want to marry?
> *Vern*: Someone who is fairly good-looking, but not too good-
> looking so she'd be out, with other people screwing her
> up. Someone who don't mind what I'm doing, let me go
> out with the guys. I won't mind if she goes out with the
> girls either. I want her to have a job so she ain't home all
> the time. 'Cause a woman goes bonkers if she's at home all
> day. Give her a job and let her get out of the house.
>   . . . People tended to get married as soon as they got out
> of school, not as soon as, but a couple of years after. I
> think people nowadays don't want to get married until
> twenty, thirty.
> *LW*: And that's because of what?
> *Vern*: They've seen too many divorces.

It is noteworthy that Vern is the only boy to discuss divorce as an impediment to marriage. Almost every girl interviewed discusses divorce, and it is a topic of conversation among young women. Despite Vern's relatively more open-minded attitude toward females, it is significant that he still envisions himself "allowing" his wife to work, and sees his role as one of controlling her time and space. He does not, for example, want her to be "too good-looking" because then she would be out, with "other people screwing her up." He also notes that he "does not mind" her going "out with the girls," and that he wants "her to have a job so she ain't home all the time."

The boy below expresses the sentiment that marriage is a "ball and chain," and that he, therefore, wants no part of it. Only a couple of the boys expressed a similar sentiment or elaborated the theme of "freedom" associated with being single. Again, this is unlike the girls.

> *Tom*: I don't want to get married; I don't want to have chil-
> dren. I want to be pretty much free. If I settle down with
> someone, it won't be through marriage.
> *LW*: Why not?
> *Tom*: Marriage is a ball and chain. Then marital problems come
> up, financial problems, whatever. I don't really want to get
> involved in them intense kind of problems between you
> and a spouse. . . . To me it's a joke.
> *LW*: Tell me why you think that.
> *Tom*: Well, I see a lot of people. I look at my father and
> mother. They don't get along, really.

The vast majority of boys at Freeway High intend to set up homes in which they exert control over their wives—in which they exit the home to engage in paid labor and their wives stay at home. Only a few question the institution of marriage, and only one begins to question a fundamental premise of patriarchy—that women's place is in the home and men's place is in the external or public sphere. As noted above, however, even this one boy sees himself largely controlling the actions of his wife. Central to the boys' identity, then, is the estab-lishment of male dominance in the home/family sphere as well as in the paid labor force. It must be understood that the construction of a male-dominant identity is absolutely dependent upon the construction of women as unable to take care of themselves monetarily and as having full responsibility for the day-to-day activities of children. Young White men strip, in a sense, the female subject. As Vern notes, he wishes to marry someone "who is fairly good looking, but not too good looking so she'd be out *with other people screwing her up*" (my emphasis).

As young White men weave their own form of material cultural superiority vis-à-vis women, they are encouraged by a larger society and societal institutions, such as schools, which concur. In this work-ing-class school, there is simply no sustained challenge to the vision of male dominance woven by male youth. Although young White working-class women challenge this vision in their own privatized fantasies about their future lives, they neither challenge the men publicly nor understand that they will have to focus their energies collectively if their private challenges to the social order have any chance of succeeding. In many cases the school actively aides in the construction of male dominance (Weis, 1990).

RACISM AND THE CONSTRUCTION OF THE "OTHER"

Freeway is a divided town, and a small number of Arabs and Hispanics live among Blacks largely on one side of the "tracks," and Whites on the other, although there are Whites living in one section of Freeway just adjacent to the steel mill, which is in the area populated by people of color. Virtually no people of color live in the White area, unlike large American cities where there are pockets of considerable mix. Most African Americans came from the South during and after World War II, drawn by the lure of jobs in the steel plant. Having been relegated to the dirtiest and lowest-paid jobs, most are now living in large public housing projects, never having been able to amass the necessary capital to live elsewhere. Although I have no evidence of this, I also assume that even had they been able to amass capital, mortgages would have been turned down if Blacks had wished to move into the White area. Also, there is no doubt informal agreements among those who rent not to rent to Blacks in the White areas. Today most project residents receive welfare and have done so for a number of years.

It is most striking that people of color are used as a foil against which acceptable moral, and particularly sexual, standards are woven among young White men. This weaves in and out of a protectionist stance taken vis-à-vis White women. The goodness of White is always contrasted with the badness of Black—Blacks are involved with drugs; Blacks are unacceptable sexually; Black men attempt to "invade" White sexual space by talking with White women; Black women are simply filthy. The boundaries of acceptable behavior are drawn, for White men, at what becomes defined as Black. Although there are numerous Black athletes at Freeway High, I never heard discussion of this among young White men. Academics are not highly valued at this school, so good Black students would not be noted either. There is a virtual denial of anything at all good being identified with Blackness. White masculinity, then, is constructed *by* White men, both in relation to

Black men and Black women, and White women. How these groups intersect in this construction will be explored below. Once again, as with White women, discursive messages in the larger society as well as those filtered through the institution itself have a hand in shaping these constructions. They are not woven solely through the thinness of peer interactions, disconnected from historically rooted societal constructions. On the contrary, although it is not my intention to explore this issue here. Much of the expressed racism in this class fraction centers around "access" to women, thus serving the dual purpose of constructing Blacks *and* White women:

> *Jim*: The minorities are really bad into drugs. You're talking everything. Anything you want, you get from them. A prime example, the ———— ward of Freeway; about twenty years ago the ———— ward was predominantly White, my grandfather used to live there. Then Italians, Polish, the Irish people, everything was fine. The houses were maintained; there was a good standard of living. . . .
>
> . . . The Blacks brought drugs. I'm not saying White people didn't have drugs; they had drugs, but to a certain extent. But drugs were like a social thing. But now you go down to the ward; it's amazing, it's a ghetto. Some of the houses are okay. They try to keep them up. Most of the homes are really, really terrible. They throw garbage on the front lawn; it's sickening. You talk to people from [surrounding suburbs]. Anywhere you talk to people, they tend to think the majority of our school is Black. They think you hang with Black people, listen to Black music.
>
> . . . A few of them [Blacks] are starting to go into the ————ward now [the White side], so they're moving around. My parents will be around there when that happens, but I'd like to be out of there.

*   *   *

> *LW*: There's no fighting and stuff here [school], is there?
> *Clint*: Yeah, a lot between Blacks and Whites.
> *LW*: Who starts them?
> *Clint*: Blacks.

LW: Do Blacks and Whites hang out in the same place?

Clint: Some do; [the Blacks] live on the other side of town. . . .
A lot of it [fights] starts with Blacks messing with White
girls. That's how a lot of them start. Even if they [White
guys] don't like the White girl, they don't like to see . . .

LW: How do you feel about that yourself?

Clint: I don't like it. If I catch them [Blacks] near my sister,
they'll get it. I don't like to see it like that. Most of them
[my friends] see it that way [the same way he does].

LW: Do you think the girls encourage the attentions of these
Black guys?

Clint: Naw. I think the Blacks just make themselves at home.
They welcome themselves in.

LW: How about the other way around? White guys and Black
girls?

Clint: There's a few that do. There's people that I know of, but
no one I hang around with. I don't know many White kids
that date Black girls.

*   *   *

Bill: Like my brother, he's in ninth grade. He's in trouble all
the time. Last year he got jumped in school. . . . About his
girlfriend. He don't like Blacks. They come up to her and
go, "Nice ass," and all that shit. My brother don't like that
when they call her "nice ass" and stuff like that. He got
suspended for saying "fucking nigger"; but it's all right for
a Black guy to go up to Whites and say stuff like that
["nice ass"]. . . . Sometime the principals aren't doing their
job. Like when my brother told [the assistant principal]
that something is going to happen, Mr. ——— just said,
"Leave it alone, just turn your head"
. . . Like they [administrators] don't know when fights
start in this school. Like there's this one guy's little sister, a
nigger [correction]—a Black guy grabbed her ass. He hit
him a couple of times. Did the principal know about it?
No!

LW: What if a White guy did that [grabbed the girl's ass]?

Bill: He'd probably have punched him. But a lot of it's 'cause they're Black.

It is important to note in the above the ways in which several discursive separations are occurring. To begin with, once again, White men are constructing women as people who need the protection of men. The young men are willing to fight for their young women so that if anyone says "nice ass," it is legitimate to start a fight. Black men, in turn, are being constructed as overly sexualized. They "welcome themselves in"; they behave in ways that are inappropriate vis-à-vis White women. It is very important here that the complaint is about intruding onto White property. It is not only that women are being defended from the inappropriate advances of oversexualized Blacks. Rather, it is the fact that *Black men are invading the property of White men that is at issue here.* Furthermore, the discursive construction of Black men as oversexualized enables White men to elaborate their own appropriate heterosexuality. By engaging in this discursive construction of Black men, they are asserting their *own* heterosexism and what they see as appropriate homophobia, since only heterosexual men presumably would be threatened by this form of intrusion. Thus, at a time of heightened concern with homosexuality (by virtue of their age and the collective nature of their lives), these boys can assert virulently and publicly their concern with Black men, thus expressing their own appropriate sexuality as well as their ability to "take care of their women." There is a grotesqueness about this particular set of interactions, a grotesqueness that enables White men to continue to define themselves as pure and straight, while defining Black men as dirty and oversexualized. The White female can then be, once again, put on a pedestal (read, stripped of her subject), although their own behavior certainly contradicts this place for White women. It is most interesting that not one White female ever constructed young Black men as a "problem" in this regard. This is not to say that White females are not racist, but this discursive rendering of Blacks is quite noticeably under the cultural terrain of White men, at least at this age. If one accepts that these men are constructing themselves as providers and protectors of White women, then it is arguably the case that they are also constructing for women the discursive rendering of Blacks described here. The young women, in turn, have no particular discursive rendering of Blacks at all.

Observational data support the notion of racism among White youth. This is mainly directed toward Blacks, although, as the excerpts below indicate, racism surfaces with respect to Arabs as well. There is a small population of Yemenites who emigrated to Freeway to work in the steel mills, and this group is targeted to some extent also.

Social Studies, November 26, 1986

Sam: Hey, Abdul, did you come from Arabia?
Abdul: Yeah.
Sam: How did you get here?
Abdul: I walked.
Sam: No, seriously, how'd you get here?
Abdul: Boat.
Sam: Where'd you come from?
Abdul: Saudi Arabia.
Sam: We don't want you. Why don't you go back.
[no comment]

Social Studies, December 11, 1986

Ed: Do you party, Nabil?
Nabil: Yeah.
Paul: Nabil, the only thing you know how to play is polo on
     camels.
[Nabil ignores]

English, October 2, 1986

LW: [To Terry, who was hit by a car two days ago]. How are
     you?
Terry: Look at me [sic] face. Ain't it cool? [He was all scraped
     up.]
LW: What happened?
Terry: Some stupid camel jockey ran me over in a big white
     car. Arabian dude.

Most of the virulent racism is directed toward Blacks, however. The word "nigger" flows freely from the lips of White males, and they treat Black females far worse than they say Black males treat White females.

At the Lunch Table, February 21, 1986

[discussion with Craig Centrie, research assistant]
Pete: Why is it [your leather bag] so big?
Mike: So he can carry lots of stuff.
CC: Yes, I bought it because my passport would fit in it.
Pete: Passport! Wow—where are you from?
CC: Well, I'm American now, but you need one to travel.
Pete: Can I see? [He pulls out his passport. Everyone looks.]
Mike: This is my first time to ever see one. What are all these
    stamps?
CC: Those are admissions stamps so [you] can get in and out
    of countries.
Mike: Look, Pete, N-I-G-E-R-I-A [pronounced Niggeria]. Yo-
    landa [a Black female] should go there. [Everyone laughs.]
Pete: [Did you see any] crocodile-eating niggers? [laughter]

In the Lunchroom, January 21, 1986

Students [all White males at the table] joke about cafeteria food.
They then begin to talk about Martin Luther King Day.
Dave: I have a wet dream—about little White boys and little
    Black girls. [laughter]

In the Lunchroom, March 7, 1986

Once again, in lunch, everyone complains about the food. Vern
asked about a party he heard about. Everyone knew about it,
but it wasn't clear where it would be. A kid walked past the table [of White boys].
Clint: That's the motherfucker. I'll whoop his ass. [The entire ta-
    ble goes "ou' ou' ou.'"]
CC: What happened with those tickets, Pete? [Some dance tick-
    ets had been stolen.]
Pete: Nothing, but I'm pissed off at that nigger that blamed me.
Pete forgot how loud he was speaking and looked toward Yolanda [a Black female] to see if she reacted. But she hadn't
heard the remark.

At the Lunch Table, February 12, 1986

Mike: That nigger makes me sick.
Pete: Who?
Mike: You know, Yolanda.
Pete: She's just right for you, man.
Mike: Not me, maybe Clint.

At the Lunch Table, February 12, 1986

About 2 minutes later, Darcy [a Black female] calls me [CC] over.
Darcy: "What's your name?"
CC: Craig, what's yours?
Darcy: It's Darcy. Clint told me a lie. He said your name was Joe. Why don't you come to a party at Yolanda's house to-night?
Yolanda: Why don't you just tell him you want him to come [everyone laughs].
Clint: Well, *all right*, they want you!
Pete: What do you think of Yolanda?
CC: She's a nice girl. What do you think?
Pete: She's a stuck-up nigger. Be sure to write that down.

*   *   *

[A group of males talk about themselves.] "We like to party all the time and get high!" [They call themselves "freaks" and "heads."] [About Blacks:] "They are a group unto themselves. They are all bullshitters."

At the Lunch Table, February 12, 1986

Much of the time, students discussed the food. Vern talked about the Valentine's Day dance and began discussing getting stoned before the dance.
CC: Do you guys drink at the dance, too?
Pete: No, I don't know what they would do to us [everyone laughs]. There probably wouldn't be any more dances.

[Yolanda and friends walk in. Yolanda and a friend were wear-
　　ing exactly the same outfit.]
Clint: What are you two—the fucking Gold Dust Twins?
Yolanda: Shut the fuck up, "boy" [everyone laughs].
[Quietly, Pete says, "Craig, they are nasty."]
CC: What do you mean?
Pete: You don't understand Black people. They're yeach. They
　　smell funny and they [got] hair under their arms.
[Clint, Pete, Mike, and Jack all make noises to denote disgust.]

The males spend a great deal of time exhibiting disgust for racial
minorities, and at the same time, asserting a protective stance over
White females vis-à-vis Black males. They differentiate themselves
from Black males and females in different ways, however. Black males
are treated with anger for invading *their* property (White girls). Black
females, on the other hand, are treated with simple disgust. Both are
seen and interacted with largely in the sexual realm, however, albeit
for different reasons and in different ways.

It is also significant that White males elaborated upon sex largely
in relation to Blacks. Certainly their own identity is bound up with
sexuality but this sexuality comes through most vehemently and consistently in relation to Black males and females. They use sexuality as
a means of "trashing" Black males and females, and setting themselves
up as "different from" them in the sexual realm. Thus Black sexual
behavior, both male and female, is seen as being inappropriate—unlike
their own. While sexuality is certainly elaborated upon in relation to
White girls (and obviously encoded in discussions about children),
such discussions do not exhibit the same ugliness as those involving
Blacks and the constructed sexuality of Blacks. It is significant, for
example, that when a group of White males was discussing Martin
Luther King Day, they said, "I have a wet dream—'bout little White
boys and little Black girls." It is even more significant that Pete said,
"You don't understand Black people. They're yeach. They smell funny
and they [got] hair under their arms." Blacks are talked about largely
in terms of sexuality, and sexuality is talked about to a great extent
in terms of Blacks. Blacks are used to demonstrate the boundaries of
acceptable sexual behavior (in that Black behavior is unacceptable)
and provide a means of enabling Whites to set themselves up as
"better than" (more responsible, less dirty, and so forth) in this area.

Although White boys do say, as I noted above, "nice ass" to White girls, they do not see this as contradictory to their embedded attitudes toward Black sexuality, given that they feel that White girls are their property to begin with. Black sexuality is simply negative; their own sexuality is, in turn, seen as positive. *In the final analysis, White males elaborate an identity in relation to the ideologically constructed identity of both Black male and Black female.* In other words, White males elaborate their own identity in relation to the identity that they construct *for* others, in this case, Black male and Black female. In so doing, they set themselves up as "other than" and "better than" each group.

Young White men spend a great deal of time expressing and exhibiting disgust for people of color. This is done at the same time as they elaborate an uninvited protective stance toward White women. In a sense, these young men "are inviting themselves in" to White women's lives in the way that they accuse Black men of "inviting themselves in" to these same young women's lives. Of course, for the White men they draw the bounds of acceptability at their own actions, denoting as unacceptable the ways in which they envision Black men "inviting themselves in." Their discursive rendering of Blacks takes a distinctly genderized form. Black males are treated with contempt for invading their property (White girls), thus enabling these men to draw distinctions between their own sexual behavior and that of Blacks, as well as drawing themselves out as coming to the aid of the "damsel in distress." In addition, these episodes enable a discursive rendering of themselves as *definitely* heterosexual. Black females are treated with simple disgust; seen as beyond the boundaries of what is an acceptable heterosexual object at one and the same time as Black women are set up as "something" that anyone can do anything with sexually because they are beyond the limits of acceptable sexual practice (witness the Martin Luther King "chant").

It is significant that young White men elaborate their own sexuality largely in relation to Blacks. Black men and women are the foil against which they set up their own heterosexuality as well as their own ultimate desire for stable two-parent families. White women are, on the other hand, largely talked about in terms of family and children. While there are certainly gross discussions about young White women as well, these pale in contrast to the discussions about Black women. Blacks are used largely to express contempt and, at the same time, encourage young White men to set themselves up as "pure" in relation to people of color. "I have a wet dream—about little White boys and little Black girls" undermines the seriousness of the Black struggle, turning it filthy. Thus, when young White working-class men say "nice ass" to White girls, it is okay, because it is somehow different than when Blacks do it. Also, of course, White women are seen as the property of White men, therefore making it all the more acceptable for them to say and do anything they like.

CONCLUSION

In this essay I have traced the drawing of "other" as young White working-class men form their own racial, class, and gendered identity. In order to form themselves as White and male, they simultaneously construct the White female "other" as well as the Black male and female "other." Their own construction of self is intimately bound up with the discursive construction of "other." The ways in which these types of constructions take place are critically important. For the White working-class male, at least in this particular sector of the country, the construction of Blacks takes on central importance. Ultimately, these young White men will enter adulthood with very racist constructions of people of color which they created (in relation, of course, to the material and discursive constructions of people of color in the society at large). Such constructions will be difficult to dislodge, particularly since they are so intimately braided with their own sexuality. While certainly later experiences in the workforce and so forth, will layer on top of this, perhaps altering it a bit (or reinforcing it through similar constructions in adult life), we must take pause at the real meaning of sexism and racism and their depth when this occurs. This is not, of course, to deny the very real material issues surrounding racism and sexism in this country. However, discursive constructions are key, as Michel Foucault argues. They set limits on what is imagined as possible. Listening to the voices of young White working-class men pries open a reality of racism, in particular, and the ways in which racism is linked to expressed heterosexuality and male dominance for Whites that may be far deeper than we imagined. As scholars dedicated to the opening up of democratic public space, we certainly have our work cut out for us.

POSTSCRIPT

Working Class Without Work (Weis, 1990), the broader study from which the previous chapter was constructed, probes the identity formation processes among White working-class male and female students in relation to the school, economy, and family of origin, capturing the complex relations among schooling, human agency, and the formation of collective consciousness within a radically changed economic context. Lois argues in the larger study that the young women exhibit a glimmer of critique regarding the traditional gender order embedded in their community, and that the young men, in line with what you read in Chapter 3, are ripe for new right consciousness given their strident racism and male-dominant stance in an economy that offers them little. While students and their parents recognize the rising certification aspect of education if they are to compete for jobs outside of traditional industry, a sector of the economy that is rapidly disappearing, education carried little intrinsic importance, and its instrumentality is evident among both the teachers and the students. Teachers are mainly concerned with rote memorization and students concerned with "passing" courses, often through cheating.

In the chapter that follows, you will see that the school contributes directly and consistently to these outcomes. Through disciplinary technologies (Davidson, 1996), internal sorting mechanisms, and messages distributed through both the formal and informal or "hidden curriculum," the school plays a key role in the reproduction of social class inequalities as well as the production of forms of consciousness linked to sensibilities around social class, race, gender, and sexuality.

What follows should not be read as a wholly idiosyncratic moment in American public schooling—something that *only* happened in this particular school. Rather, the activities and interactions chronicled in Chapter 4 must be seen as "what can happen" if race, class, and gender hierarchical arrangements are left uninterrupted.

Acquiring White Working-Class Identities: Legitimate and Silenced Discourse within the School

Lois Weis

September 9, 1985: 4th Period Study Hall

(the second day of school)

Mr. Paul: Okay. This is a study hall. That's what I expect you to do.

Joe: Only a hundred and seventy-eight more days until the end of the year [to the guy next to him].

Mr. Paul: You're not the only one counting. How many days?

Joe: A hundred and seventy-eight.

Mr. Paul: How many hours?

Joe: Let me see [he figures it out]. One thousand four hundred twenty-four more periods.

Mr. Paul: One thousand four hundred twenty-four hours?

Joe: No, periods. We don't want too much specificity. . . . We are now into the second full day of our education [everyone was laughing].

Chapter 4 previously appeared in *Working Class without Work: High School Students in a De-Industrializing Economy*, by Lois Weis (pp. 80–115), copyright © 1990. Reproduced by permission of Routledge, Inc., part of The Taylor and Francis Group.

The question arises, What does the school do to encourage and/ or block the formation of the identities such as those outlined in Chapter 3? To what extent is the school complicit in the production of the racist, sexist, and homophobic attitudes and behaviors we witnessed among the Freeway boys in the previous chapter? Here I explore elements of school culture and speculate as to possible effects on student identities.

I will argue two major points here. First, I will suggest that the school embodies and promotes a contradictory attitude toward schooling and school knowledge, with a stress on the form of schooling rather than the substance of learning. Second, I will suggest that the school, through its routine practices, serves to encourage the maintenance of separate identities along gender and race lines, thus encouraging, perhaps unintentionally, the construction of "other" discussed in the last chapter. At the same time, again, perhaps unintentionally, Freeway High encourages the notion that White-male identity is superior to all others.

CONTRADICTIONS WITH RESPECT TO EDUCATION

Freeway High classes embody the same contradictory code of respect toward knowledge and schooling as is embedded within the identities of its youth. Teachers tend to adhere to the form rather than the substance of education, and knowledge tends to be flat and prepackaged. This is reminiscent of curriculum described by Linda McNeil (1981) in her high school study, and Jean Anyon (1982) in her study of knowledge as distributed through the working-class elementary school. On the one hand, education in Freeway is articulated in highly instrumental terms as positive by teachers—it leads to a better job and so forth. This, again, is much the same way in which the students themselves see it. On the other hand, knowledge distributed through the classes has nothing to do with either thinking or challenging (Anyon, 1981; McNeil, 1986).

Teachers almost uniformly suggest that education is necessary to obtain what they consider to be reasonable employment. This comes through in their conversations with me alone as well as in their verbal classroom posture.

January 16: Social Studies

A long explanation of the electoral system; national nominating convention; campaigns; and elections. Mr. Sykes then hands out a work sheet on the topic. "Answer the five questions on the bottom. I'll see if you understand everything. Take about ten minutes."

"If the steel plant were still open you guys wouldn't have to worry about this. You could crawl into some coil for an eight-hour shift and fall asleep and still get paid for it. That's probably one of the reasons why the plant closed." Mr. Sykes walks around. "Do you guys take math? You guys are terrible in math. This is simple addition. You want my calculator?"

October 30: Social Studies

Mr. Simon: Why does level of education prevent you from getting a job? Okay. If there are a hundred jobs on a page in the want ads, ten percent of these, you need an elementary education; forty percent of these jobs you heed a high school education; forty percent you need a college education; ten percent of these jobs you need a college plus [education].

The door system works as follows: If you have an elementary education, you can knock on ten doors. If you have a high school education, you can knock on fifty doors. If you have a college plus, you can knock on one hundred doors. Each time you have a piece of paper, you can knock on more doors. Each time you get more education, you can *try* [emphasis his] for more jobs. If you have college plus, you may not get a job, but your chances are going to be better.

The people who live in the poor parts of town have less education and it is more difficult for them to get jobs.

While teachers let students know that they feel that schooling is useful in instrumental terms, there is, in fact, little importance given to the real substance of schooling. The knowledge form is, indeed, very telling, with virtually all classes taking the form of top-down distribution of knowledge. While this may not be particularly unusual, and several studies have pointed to the same phenomenon in the American school, the situation in Freeway is extreme. Teachers tend to tell students *exactly* what to put in their notebooks, for example, down to the outline format and where to place commas. Thus, it is not only a matter of students outlining information presented in a textbook, for instance, as has been documented in a number of other studies. Teachers actually control the *very form of the outline* and students are not encouraged to make the information their own even at the point of transferring it into their notebooks. This form of knowledge distribution is highly routinized in Freeway High and only one class, the advanced social studies class, broke out of it in all the classes I observed. The following classroom observations clarify my point. It is extremely significant that student question posing took *only* the form of asking for clarification of directions. At only one point during the entire year did I see evidence, outside of the advanced class, of students posing questions about and/or challenges to the knowledge itself. In fairness to the students, however, the form of knowledge distributed through the classroom does not leave much room for interaction with that knowledge. In fairness to the teachers, it may not make any difference even if it does.

November 12: English

    Mr. Kindley: Part of the exam we take in June is the listening exercise. There is no reason why you can't get eight or nine on the [state external] exam. There is no way you can really study for this, but we can get used to the questions.

        This is not a reading exercise. Nowhere on the exam are you going to find what I read to you. I'm going to read a passage to you. Then I'll tell you where to look for the questions.

        [He reads a passage about Bulgaria's Communist Party. We then look at the questions in the book and he rereads the passage.]

        Don't look at the passage in the book; you won't have a passage to read in June. Now, you have five minutes to put your answers down.

The above simply reflects intense preparation on the part of the teacher for the state external exam to be taken in June, an exam that all students in this class must take due to new state regulations. In that sense, the above description is not striking—many schools might look similar. What is important, however, is Mr. Kindley's follow-up discussion on taking a listening test below. The precision with which he instructs students *how* to place the notes in their notebooks is key here.

> *Mr. Kindley:* Okay. Open up to page eleven [in the textbook] and get your notebooks out. Skip a line and write "Listening Test—suggestions on how to use your time." There are four steps involved with this.
>
> Roman numeral one in your notes. Write down, "During the first reading." Number one. "Listen to the topic, usually stated in the first two sentences, and for the supporting details. Pay close attention to the conclusion which often stresses the main ideas." [This is *directly* from the book.]
>
> Roman numeral two. "During your reading of the questions," and [write down] just what it has on our page eleven there, "your primary goal at this time is to become as aware as possible of all the questions so you will know the specific information to listen for."
>
> Roman numeral three, next page, page twelve, "During the second reading, the two things you are asked to do at this time are to listen to the passage and to write the answers. Of the two, the listening is the most important. You must keep listening." Underline the last sentence.

The point here is that notes are given in extreme detail, including what to underline, where to place commas, and so forth. This was not idiosyncratic but occurred in a number of classes.

October 24: Social Studies

> *Mr. Sykes:* Put down in your notes, "Unit one, part four." Put down "Four disadvantaged" [he spells] "groups in the population."

Jim: For?

Jerry: What do we got to write after that?

Mr. Sykes: Page sixty-six [referring to text]. Just list them.
Number 1. The American Indian.
Number 2. Hispanic Americans.
Number 3. American women, page eighty-seven.

Jim: American broads.

Mr. Sykes: [He ignores the comment on "broads."] Number
four. American blacks, page one hundred five.

October 30: Social Studies

Mr. Simon: Page sixteen. Take out your notebooks.
The title. "The Reasons for the Growth of Cities." Put
that down. It is at the bottom of page sixty.
A. Industrial Revolution
Skip a line. Take the next subtitle [from the text]. "B.
Problems Facing Cities and Urban Populations." Take the
next five subtopics under that. Skip a line between each.

Joe: Just one line between each?

Mr. Simon: Yes.

Sam: Just the five?

Mr. Simon: Yes. The public health department has two main
functions: one, enforcing health codes; and two, to aid, as-
sist and help those people who do get sick and cannot afford it.
Put down the functions [in your notes] and then put
down a "dash"; then put down "money" and a question
mark.

The distribution of knowledge in Freeway High is highly routinized. Students write down in their notebooks prepackaged notes that
teachers deliver to them, and students are tested on these notes at a
later time. At no point in this process is there any discussion, much
less serious discussion, of the ideas or concepts embedded within the
original materials.

Obviously, I could not observe all classes in the high school, and
questions may be raised with respect to the representativeness of what
I found. However, it is striking that in all the classes visited over the
year by myself and two graduate assistants (this would add up to

hundreds of class sessions spread throughout the curriculum), it is only in the advanced class that knowledge took on a form different from that outlined here. This goes even further than the lamentable situation found by Michael Apple, Linda McNeil, and Jean Anyon in previous studies, and must be understood as linked to the social class of the students (see Anyon, 1981; McNeil, 1986; Apple, 1979, 1983). While there may be individual classes in Freeway High that operate differently and were missed in the ethnography, there is absolutely no question that the form reported here is the norm.

Even in the case of the question raised by Mr. Simon above regarding whether the state is able to support public health, there was *never* any discussion of this issue. It was simply a point in the prepackaged notes suggested by a "dash," the word "money," and a question mark. Students had no idea what was meant by this or, perhaps even worse, any interest in knowing. When students ask questions, they are almost always for the purpose of clarification. Such questions are not for the purpose of clarifying ideas, however, but the form of the notes themselves, as the following example suggests:

Teacher: You have two assignments today. Rewrite the last one to correct your mistakes. Also, start question three. Read the entire question first. Find out what the question asks, then answer the question.

Male Student: Do we have to write the question? [In other words, when we provide the answer, do we have to write down the question first?]

Teacher: Yes.

*   *   *

Teacher: Page seven. We populated the thirteen colonies.

Male Student: Should we write that down [in our notebooks?]

Teacher: No, not until you read it.

Student questions almost always take the form of asking for clarification of minor points related to directions: whether to add a dash or not in the notes, answer this or that question, skip one or two lines, and so forth. It is not a questioning that revolves around clarification of ideas, much less a challenge to such ideas. In the year I was in

Freeway (I attended classes 3 days a week), I witnessed only one challenge to an idea in a nonadvanced class, and many more such challenges in an advanced social studies class. Interestingly enough, the one challenge in the nonadvanced class centered on knowledge about alcoholism, as did one of the most well-articulated challenges to teacher knowledge in an advanced class. Since drinking is seen by students as *their* knowledge, it is, therefore, significant that challenges emerge in this area. The first observation comes from a nonadvanced English class; the second, an advanced social studies class.

October 23: English

Mr. Kindley: Okay, take out your notebooks. In your notes, just skip a line from where you were. Number one. *High and Outside*. Author is Linda A. Dove. Setting: A town near San Francisco.

He proceeds to give them notes from the entire book, including characters, plot, and so forth, even though they read the book. [The form of "reading" the book was orally in class.]

Mr. Kindley: Skip another line and we get into Carl Etchen, Niki's father, who has treated her like an adult from the age of fourteen by including her in his wine tasting and afternoon cocktail hours. He was trying to protect her from the wild party drinking of other teenagers. But he unwittingly *caused* [my emphasis] her alcoholism.

Holly: How did he cause her alcoholism? [with skepticism; indicating that she understood that alcoholism is a disease and that one person cannot cause it to occur in another].

Mr. Kindley: I know what you're trying to say. What we're trying to do here is get some notes for the end of the year [state exams]. Maybe I should change the word "cause."

Holly: No, no.

Mr. Kindley: No, you're making a good point.

It is interesting that Holly had a difficult time sustaining her challenge to teacher knowledge, even though the subject was not unfamiliar to her. When Mr. Kindley said he should "change the word 'cause,'" her comment was "No, no," suggesting that she didn't really want to enter into such a challenge at all, however minor it was.

The following observation suggests a more sustained challenge on the same subject from an advanced student:

March 4, Social Studies

An interesting discussion on drinking. It started out as a discussion about the lawmaking process and it turned into a discussion about the 21-year-old drinking age in the state.

Suzanne: Why penalize young people? There are plenty of men over forty who get drunk all the time.

Mr. Mouton: Yeah, but they don't go *out* [emphasis his] to get drunk. They don't say, "Hey, it's Friday let's go out and get bombed." Adults don't do that.

Suzanne: Sure they do. They do it all the time.

Mr. Mouton: I can name twenty-five kids; you name two adults.

Suzanne: My dad.

Mr. Mouton: Does he get drunk?

Suzanne: Yeah.

Mr. Mouton: How often?

Suzanne: Three times a week.

Mr. Mouton: Oh, name another.

Suzanne: We own a bar. There are plenty of guys who come in night after night and get bombed. I work there. I see the same guys all the time.

It is significant that the minor challenge I witnessed to teacher knowledge in the nonadvanced class had to do with a subject students feel is their own—drinking. The second challenge, noted above, is much more sustained than the first and also revolves around drinking. The main point here is that there are virtually *no* questions and/or challenges raised to school-based knowledge in nonadvanced classes. The form of knowledge itself did not encourage such challenge and/or questions, of course, and the students did not take them up on their own. There were, however, some challenges expressed in the advanced social studies class throughout the year. Here knowledge was more open to begin with, and therefore, more accessible to true discussion. It must be remembered, however, that only 25 students take the advanced curriculum out of the entire junior class in a large urban-area high school.

Although there are some minimal challenges by teachers to curricular form as expressed in the district, knowledge, as distributed through this working-class school, largely fits the model of knowledge described by Jean Anyon (1982). As such, "A large portion of what the children were asked [revolved around carrying] out procedures, the purposes of which were often unexplained, and which were seemingly unconnected to thought processes or decision making of their own." An example, according to Anyon, of this type of instruction

> was when one of the fifth-grade teachers led the children through a series of steps to make a one-inch grid on their papers without telling them that they were making a one-inch grid or that it would be used to study scale. She said, "Take your ruler. Put it across the top. Make a mark at every number. Then move your ruler down the bottom. Now, put it across the bottom. Now make a mark on top of every number. Now draw a line from . . . " At this point, one student said she had a faster way to do it and the teacher said, "No, you don't; you don't even know what I'm making yet. Do it this way or it's wrong." (1982, p. 8)

The form of knowledge distributed through Freeway parallels that described in Anyon's working-class schools. In her schools, students did not envision knowledge as "thinking" but spoke in terms of behaviors or skills. Knowledge was something, even in fifth grade, that one "acquired" from authorities. One did not interact with it, much less challenge or create it. The Freeway school exhibits similar characteristics. Teachers simply perfected a further prepackaging of the distribution of knowledge, and students perfected the appearance of the passive "absorption" of it. In many cases, they did not even "absorb" it, however, as test data show. In fact, neither group, teachers or students, was involved in their part of the equation other than at the level of ritual, and both were highly alienated from the process and the product. Teachers engaged in the "packaging" of knowledge and students engaged in the passive "acquiring" of it. Students challenge the school virtually not at all, whether in the realm of knowledge or otherwise. They just hope to get *through* it by "passing" and are willing to sit quietly in order to get Cs. Herein the contradictory attitude toward knowledge and school culture can be seen. Both teachers and students engage in a highly routinized *form* of knowledge, but not in its substance. Indeed, the form *is* the curriculum in a sense, since no other curriculum is really available. Neither teachers nor students move beyond this established ritual in the classroom. At the same time, both groups agree that school is important, in the sense that the *credential* is important, thus bringing the contradictory code of respect toward education squarely into the site of the high school.

It is important to note here that it is not knowledge itself that emerges as key, but the diploma. The diploma can be obtained whether one questions and/or challenges knowledge [either teachers or students] or not. In other words, one can be alienated and still obtain the short-term instrumental rewards of participating in high school. What this means in the long run is, of course, debatable. It must be noted, however, that the form of knowledge detailed here will *not* enable students to do well on the SAT (the college entrance examination) since the SAT calls for analysis, synthesis, and evaluation of high-culture material, none of which Freeway students are being trained to do. Thus, Freeway students are simply not receiving an education that will enable them to obtain entrance into 4-year colleges and universities, and get the type of jobs that will allow them, in the future, to set up middle-class lifestyles. They are, for all practical purposes, being prepared directly by the school to assume working-class positions. This is particularly problematic given the demise of the industrial proletariat, the sector of the economy in which their parents and grandparents have labored.

What is important here is that the *school itself* encourages the emerging contradictory attitude toward school culture and knowledge that is in evidence among youth both by stressing the utility of schooling and by distributing a form of knowledge that predominately serves to maintain order. Knowledge is flat and highly controlled within the school—thus divorced from the true experiences of adolescents—and the school simply demands passivity in its face in order to "pass." In this sense, then, the school acts directly to encourage some aspect of emerging White working-class identity. As noted earlier, although a contradictory code of respect toward education exists within the broader class culture, it has surfaced in the past only after workers experience the true brutality of labor. The Freeway case reflects the way in which working-class social identity is changing in this regard.

SEPARATE SPHERES

A second set of messages in the school revolves around the appropriateness of separate gender and race spheres, and the normality of certain types of behaviors and attitudes related to this separation. Such separatism is clearly a part of the identities discussed in the last chapter. The school, however, is not neutral here. Rather, the high school legitimates such separatism through its own set of routines and rituals. This is true both for gender and race, although there are countervailing tendencies within the school with respect to gender. I will address the issue of gender first.

To begin with, it is important to note that separate gender space exists in the school and that men invade female space, whereas women never invade male space. This parallels within the school the traditional allocation of space whereby men come and go from the domestic scene (women's space) but women are expected to remain in this sphere and are not welcome in public male places.[1] This use of space within the school was apparent to me when I made initial contacts with teachers in the spring of 1985 and was reinforced at the faculty in-service on September 3. Men and women simply occupy different space within the school. The faculty lounges [not simply bathrooms] are physically separate, and the faculty lunchroom is separated by virtue of where people choose to sit.

May 21, 1985: On Entering the Field

Meetings with Ms. Hartle and Ms. Jones, both of the business department. Meeting separately with Ms. Hartle at 1:15 and Mrs. Jones at 2:20. The meetings were set up by Mr. Jackson, co-ordinator of the business department, since they could not attend the general meeting for business faculty.

This is the first time I was in the faculty lounge [located down the hall from the principal's office]. The lounge is separate for men and women. The women have their side and the men theirs. When I inquired about this, Ms. Hartle said, "Yeah, that gives us more privacy. We have a rest room on each side." I asked if people ever go into the other side and she said, "The guys sometimes come here if they want to see someone, but we

never go to the other side. They come in and talk." [The men
are using the door to the women's side of the lounge even
though they have their own door.]

This same segregated pattern was apparent at the first orientation
meeting in the fall.

September 3

The orientation was scheduled to begin at 9:00. I arrived at 8:45
and there were coffee and donuts in the cafeteria. Many people
were already there. Personnel tended to be gender segregated.
Men were at their own tables, and women theirs. It was immediately apparent that this was the case.

Throughout the school year, these patterns persisted. Although
there were separate spaces for women and men, it was seen as acceptable that men invaded women's space. Men constantly walked into
the women's side of the lounge and sat and talked, for example.
Conversely, I never saw a woman in the men's lounge, and it would
have been seen as highly unacceptable. I myself was made to feel that
the men's lounge was not my space, although the women's lounge
was theirs. The lunchroom, although ostensibly shared gender space,
once again was divided. Only one female, a math teacher, regularly
sat with men, and only one male, a social studies teacher, regularly
sat with women. The one African-American female teacher in the
lunch period I joined on a regular basis, sat with the monitors, some
of whom are African-American and some White. The White females
always sit at one end of the table, the women of color and all monitors
and aides sit at the other end of the "female table." This was a stable
seating pattern throughout the entire year, and tended to be reflected
in all other lunch periods, although I spent most of my time in one
of them.

Interactions within the spaces tended to be stereotypically gender
specific. Women, for example, often discussed recipes, food, cosmetics,
and so forth. Men discussed, on the other hand, computers, football,
and betting pools. Significantly, little of the lunchroom talk revolved
around students, although there is talk, as noted earlier, about the

administration. The stereotypical nature of female discussion is evident in field notes reproduced below:

February 6, 1986: In the Lunchroom

I just realized how much of the time women teachers discuss recipes. One woman had the school lunch of chili.

Ms. Fletcher: There is too much meat in it.

Ms. Butcher: Everyone makes chili differently, I put a lot of celery and beans in it. Some people don't.

Ms. Fletcher: I do, too. This chili has too much meat in it.

Ms. Butcher: My husband likes chili soup. He likes it so thin it's like soup. My kids call it hamburger soup. "When are you going to make hamburger soup, Mom?"

Ms. Sanford: You know, ——— [a restaurant in town] has something like a chili soup with cheese on top of it. It's good. I don't make a good chili; my daughter-in-law does. She adds a can of tomato soup at the end to thicken it. It's really good. No water, just tomato soup.

Ms. Butler: I use a can of tomatoes in mine.

At another point during the year, Ms. Snapple, the cosmetology teacher, handed out a clipping to the women in the lunchroom entitled, "Your Refrigerator Holds Worlds of Cosmetics." In this article were recipes for Avocado Dry Skin Mask, Cucumber Refresher Mask, Banana Mask, Herbal Sauna, Tomato Compress, and so forth. A great deal of time was spent by the women teachers discussing these homemade cosmetics, including what to do if you are allergic to certain fruits. Ms. Snapple pointed out that you should use the cosmetics "within a relatively short period of time, before rancidity or spoilage sets in."

In addition to recipes and related elements of traditional female culture, there are elements within this separate sphere that are directly critical of men. These range from a discussion of how sloppy men are to the fact that women still do not experience equality with males. The issue of unequal pay received quite a bit of attention from a certain group.

October 23: Lunch

Nancy [a business teacher] was talking about the salaries of secretaries. "Starting salaries in business are four thousand, nine
thousand, or ten thousand dollars. You just can't live on that.
Men come in as management trainees at seventeen thousand
dollars. Secretaries, just because they are women, don't make
seventeen thousand dollars after fifteen years. It used to make
me so mad [she was a secretary]. These men in the department
at [State University, where she used to work] used to make so
much money. I was 18 [years old] and making three thousand
nine hundred dollars. Men couldn't survive if it weren't for female secretaries."

Many other times throughout the year this conversation surfaced
among female teachers. Jan earlier said, with respect to talk about the
photocopy machines, "Yeah, and they wonder why they have teacher
shortages. We have no say over anything. They make it impossible
to do our job. The only reason that things are as good as they are is
that they've exploited bright women in the past." Nancy, a business
teacher, takes up the issue of gender inequality rather vociferously
during numerous lunch conversations and in a later interview which
I conducted with her. Below, she offers a feminist analysis of why
pay for secretaries is low, for example:

I [have had] male students say to me that they do intend to be
secretaries and they've asked, "How much do they [secretaries]
make?" Now, that's the disappointing factor since it is basically, out there in the real world, dominated by women, and
[it] is a traditional woman's occupation, its traditional pay is
low because it is not considered equal to male work and that is
a very poor perception of the males that control the corporate
world because they couldn't function without those well-
trained secretaries who sometimes may not have a college degree but have to take more specialized courses in their area
than some people at the college level and have to prove mastery. They [secretaries] are not paid for mastery in these difficult skills. The language arts and other communication skills;
the manual dexterity you need for typing and shorthand; and

just the basic decision-making skills that they have to have to be able to handle the responsibility. They do not get their just desserts at all.

There is, therefore, discussion among woman faculty of gender inequality and, particularly, low pay for women. The second point of sustained criticism among female teachers is the perception that men want female servants.

September 1985

In the teachers' lunchroom three women were complaining that it is the men [from the previous lunch period] who leave their dishes and napkins on the tables [the place is always a mess from the previous period].
Nancy: They have maids at home.
All the women were complaining that the men are slobs and don't even have the "courtesy to clean up after themselves."
Susan: They expect us to clean up after them.

May 6, 1986: In the teachers' lunchroom, 11:00

Paul [running the in-school suspension room today] is getting lunch for three students there. He is holding one tray and drops the Tater Tots [potatoes] on the floor. He proceeds to walk out.
Nancy: Did you ever notice how these guys expect someone to clean up after them?
Susan: Yeah, they really do. They leave the tables in here a mess.
Jan: I feel sorry for the girls here who get married young. They don't know what they're getting into.
Nancy: They have this knight-on-a-white-charger crap. They think they'll get a knight on a white charger, and they get a horse's ass.
Susan and Jan get up and clean up the Tater Tots from the floor.

It is noteworthy that separate spheres are maintained and, at the same time, that the female sphere contains emerging elements critical of men within it. Some of the women constantly criticize both the fact that women earn less than men, and that men expect to be picked up after. However, the women do, in fact, pick up after the men. Thus, when Paul spills the Tater Tots, Susan and Jan, although critical of male behavior, proceed to clean up. They do, in some sense then, see that as their role.

Men also invade women's space, whereas the reverse is not true, as I noted earlier. This extends to the classroom itself where, on many occasions throughout the year, I witnessed male teachers walking in and out of female classrooms to check equipment, grade papers, and so forth. It is seen as perfectly appropriate to invade women's space in this way. Conversely, I never saw a female teacher invade male space, either public in the sense of teaching space, or private in the sense of the faculty lounge.

Separate racial spheres are also maintained at Freeway High. The two African-American female faculty members, for example, always sit with the monitors and aides at lunch, some of whom are African-American, rather than with the White female teachers. Teachers often referred to the racially segregated nature of Freeway:

April 30, 1985: Entry Notes

The meeting with social studies faculty was interesting. I simply introduced myself and then let them make comments. Ms. Heyman said the students would react differently [to school] depending on the part of the city they were from. They all agreed that there were "two worlds" in Freeway. The one part has "green lawns, people who became foremen in the plant; they made it, and either moved to a certain part of Freeway or ——— [a nearby suburb]."

October 23: Social Studies class

Before the test announcement Mr. Simon was talking about integration. He said, "Is there a bridge in Freeway?"
James: Yeah.
Mr. Simon: Do Blacks live on one side of the bridge?
Rick: Yeah.
Mr. Simon: Yeah, you just don't see Blacks on this side of the bridge.
Clifton [a Black male]: You can move if you have the money.

> *Mr. Simon:* Yeah, legally you can. But your neighbors might
> not talk to you. Your children may not be allowed to play
> with the other children on the block. It's different if you
> are making a hundred thousand dollars a year.
>
> Blacks and Whites live together in those neighbor-
> hoods. Do you think anyone cares if O.J. Simpson [a well-
> known former football player] moves in next door? Hey,
> O.J.! He's famous! Oh, yeah, he's Black, but who cares?
> That's where you see the change, in the rich areas.

April 20, 1986

A school-board member walks into the teachers' lunchroom.
She is very tan, having obviously just returned from Florida or
the Caribbean. She walks up to a Black aide: "I'm as dark as
you; let's compare tans. I'll go and buy a home on ———" [in
the "Black" part of town, across the bridge].

No one would dispute that there are largely racially segregated
neighborhoods in Freeway. The large housing project "across the
tracks" is virtually all Black and Hispanic, and the area surrounding
the school—the area of "green lawns" —is entirely White. This community-based segregation is played out at the faculty level, too. There
are only three teachers of color, despite the fact that the school is
approximately 15% African-American: one Black female teaches special education, and two African-American women are in secretarial
science. The school, through its hiring practices, thus encourages separate racial spheres and reinforces the racial hierarchy. This is reflected
in lunchroom seating patterns and teacher discussion of neighborhoods, even in classrooms. Until recently, Freeway was segregated in
terms of schools; Blacks attended one set of schools and Whites another. This has, with legal action, broken down within the past 10
years, but the segregated nature of the community is still almost totally
intact. Under these circumstances, it is not surprising to find overtly
racist comments such as those below.

March 5

I went to see Johnnie Aaron [the football coach] to see if the
Nautilus room could be used for interviewing.

He said, "It's always in use; there's always someone in there."

William, a Black male student, was in Johnnie's room, as well as John, a White male.

Johnnie: What happened to your hair, "boy"?

William: It fell out. I was nervous before the game. [He shaved his head.]

Johnnie has, on other occasions, referred to Black males as "boy."

Study Hall

Anthony [a Black male]: Hi, girls [to two White girls].

Mr. Antonucci: Stop talking to White girls.

Anthony: Got any colored ones?

Mr. Antonucci: You don't seem to understand why I moved you up here [to the front]. [He kicks him out of the classroom.]

Although directly racist comments such as those above were relatively infrequent on the part of faculty, comments such as those below were not, suggesting a deep racism that lies within the teacher and school culture generally.

September 5, 1985: Talk with Mr. Weaver, the Assistant Principal.

I ran into Mr. Weaver in the hall. He was telling me what a "good system this is here. The kids are good. The [college preparation] courses are as good as the [college preparation] courses anywhere."

"This is a realistic situation here, about fifteen percent Black or minority." He thinks that if a school gets "too Black," it is no longer "serious." "Too many of their homes are giddy places, not serious enough. If you get too many Blacks in the school, it is not serious. Fifteen percent is fine. They can't act that way ['giddy'] in school if they are only fifteen percent."

The point here is not only that there are separate spaces maintained in the school through everyday rituals and activities, but that such activities and actions coupled with the distributed notion of

White male dominance encourage the virulent racism, sexism, and homophobia discussed in the previous chapter. This is not necessarily consciously directed, of course, yet the enacted separatism that exists within the school reinforces racism and, in the case of White males, the setting up of Blacks as "other" in their own constructed identity. Actions within the school also encourage the setting up of a female "other" and the assumed male dominance which accompanies this, and which rests at the very heart of the identity of White working class males. While there is some challenge to male superiority at the cultural level, these progressive elements tend to be only minimally encouraged by the school.

What goes on in Freeway is emblematic of the ways in which schools can contribute to the silencing of alternative discourses and the reproduction of fundamental inequalities and forms of consciousness associated with these inequalities, even when this is not necessarily an intended set of outcomes. Freeway students and their teachers for the most part, neither value education nor engage in it other than, at best, the level of rote memorization, thus contributing to the students' own future devalued space in the American economy. More striking though, are the ways in which the school both encourages racism, sexism and homophobia and, at the same time, offers virtually no space for collective critique, either for teachers or students. Most chilling, as we saw in Chapter 3, are the ways in which the school offers a space wherein working-class White males coconstruct their own identities in relation to those of African-American males and females, and White females.

But the school does more than offer a neutral space within which these identity productions are played out. As we see in this chapter, Freeway High, through everyday rituals and activities, actively colludes in these coconstructions, as heterosexuality, masculinity, and Whiteness emerge as distinct assertions of fierce and adversarial essentialism sustained in the face of what the young White males construct as "other" —White females and African-American males and females.

The question arises, Could it have been different? Could the school be more than a targeted site for the formation of Whiteness and space wherein this Whiteness comes to define itself in relation to the constructed negative in the other? To this, I offer a guarded "yes." Curriculum *could* be developed to expose and deconstruct assumptions surrounding Whiteness, for example. Teachers, administrators, and counselors, had they been of different sensibilities, *could* intervene and attempt to derail these coconstructions rather than reinforce them, whether intentionally or not, as we have seen here. The point is that they don't, leaving intact a set of processes that serve to center White males, marginalize others, and contribute to a set of good and bad representations that undermine the building of a multicultural and multiracial community. In Freeway's community of difference, there is active coconstruction of ugly difference, difference that lays the basis for future attack.

PART II

Scenes of Extraordinary Conversations

Over the past 20 years, scholars have amassed an impressive array of work aimed at uncovering the ways in which schools reproduce social inequalities. Forming a corpus of structuralist interpretation, such studies wind through the ways in which curriculum (Apple, 1982a; Anyon, 1983; Gaskell, 1992), standardized testing (Haney, 1993), political economy and bureaucratic organization (Anyon, 1997), teacher practices (Kelly & Nihlen, 1982), and university preparation (Ginsburg, 1988) serve to sustain broader social inequalities. Although it is well understood that schooling plays a crucial role in offering opportunities for individual social mobility, it does, at the same time, serve to perpetuate and indeed legitimize widespread structural inequalities.

Much work over the past 20 years focuses on the ways in which social inequalities along racial, social class, and gendered lines are sustained through schools. And, indeed, we have contributed writing in this area (Fine, 1993; Weis, 1990; Weis & Fine, 1993), some of which appears in the first section of this volume. Recently work has also been done on the ways in which schools inscribe heterosexuality and able-bodiedness through curriculum and social practices as well, and excellent work has been done in this regard (Barry, 2000; Fine, 1988; Friend, 1993; Sapon-Shevin, 1993; Whatley, 1991). Additional work has focused on the ways in which students themselves, through resistant cultures, further inscribe their own subordinate positions (Giroux, 1983a, 1983b; Solomon, 1992; Valli, 1986; Willis, 1977) along social class, race, gendered, and sexual lines. In the case of gender, for example, Angela McRobbie (1978) has argued persuasively that it is the girls' own culture, even more than what the school expects of girls, that ensures their (our) position in an ongoing set of patriarchal structures.

This vibrant research agenda has taken us a long way toward understanding how it is that schools sustain that which they purport to eliminate. Nevertheless, in examining the reproduction of social inequalities we may camouflage those truly outstanding moments in today's schools: instances of teachers and kids working against the grain to create more critical and egalitarian structures, to imagine more open opportunities for all, to truly challenge all that is inscribed in the American mosaic. These spaces (Katz, 1996; Keith & Pile, 1993) reflect and blend many of the commitments of critical race theorists (e.g., Delpit, 1988; Foster, 1997; Ladson-Billings, 2000; Matsuda, 1998), feminist pedagogy (Ellsworth, 1989; Lather, 1991) and resistance theorists (Giroux, 1983b; Cochran-Smith & Lytle, 1992), but with a profound sense of place and space borrowed from radical geographers such as Katz (1996), and Keith and Pile (1993). Organized to create and sustain a sense of intellectual and political community among differences, with a critical eye on power asymmetries within and outside the room, these educators have crafted rich and fragile spaces within public schools—currently sites of enormous surveillance and pressure toward reproduction. In the section that follows, we wish to honor three sites: instances of forceful pedagogy that deliberately and directly challenge inequity; sites which are sustained over time by critical educators working toward a larger political and intellectual project. We suggest, then, that these disruptions deserve critical understanding as politically and pedagogically strategic moments, within traditional schools, for identity and movement work.

What we offer here is a theoretical extension of previous work in this area. In three public schools we observe and participate with committed adults who push the boundaries of what "would be." These are educators who intentionally and self-consciously challenge the reproductive instincts of public education and create spaces in which youth can challenge"common sense" about themselves as well as others, and engage intellectual and political projects that are, indeed, counter-hegemonic. Further, these are not simply "liberatory" spaces for historically oppressed or marginalized youth, but perhaps more pedagogically treacherous, they are integrated sites in which youth with biographies of some privilege sit side by side with youth from circumstances of poverty, working for a public common understanding across lines of race, ethnicity, and geography. And finally, these educators are not simply engaged in practices of resistance, but they have designed and crafted spaces of public responsibility and intellect, carved by a racially and ethnically diverse group of educators for youths in ways that can easily (and accurately) anticipate opposition from community members, administrators, colleagues, some parents, and many youth.

In so doing, we argue that "counterpublics," such as those described by Nancy Fraser (1993) and others, can and do exist in public arenas such as schools. As the public sphere packs up and walks away from poor and working-class youth, it is absolutely essential for the community to reclaim these spaces. Those of us who work with public schools cannot sit by and accept that schools do no more than reproduce social inequalities, though this may certainly be the case much of the time. We must engage in the creation and protection of "counterpublics"—spaces where adults and youth can challenge the very exclusionary practices currently existing in public institutions— practices such as those chronicled in Part I of this volume that inscribe inequalities by social class, race, gender, and sexuality.

We have no illusions about the ease, political or pedagogical, of creating or sustaining these spaces—indeed, we are sure (and have lots of evidence) of the likely resistance. We write, instead, in this second section, with respect for the efforts that are going on and hope to join a public conversation of support for such educational practices within (not despite) the public sphere of public education, a set of practices set in juxtaposition to singular cries for high-stakes testing. As we suggest here, it is not enough to let this form of challenge go on in alternative sites, as important as these alternative sites might be (Bertram, Marusza, Fine, & Weis, 2000; Fine & Weis, 2000; Fine, Weis, Centrie, & Roberts, 2000; Morton-Christmas, 1999; Reichert, 2000). Here we focus on three projects which push against the grain: the first, a detracked ninth-grade social studies class in Montclair, New Jersey; the second, a voluntary girls group which meets in an urban magnet school in Buffalo; and the third, a middle school oral history project.

Before the Bleach Gets Us All

MICHELLE FINE, BERNADETTE ANAND,
CARLTON JORDAN, AND DANA SHERMAN

To sum up this: theoretically, the Negro needs neither separate nor mixed schools. What he needs is Education. What he must remember is that there is no magic either in mixed schools or segregated schools. A mixed school with poor unsympathetic teachers, with hostile public opinion, and no teaching of the truth concerning black folks is bad. A segregated school with ignorant placeholders, inadequate equipment, and poor salaries is equally bad. Other things being equal, the mixed school is the broader, more natural basis for the education of all youth. It gives wider contacts; it inspires greater self-confidence, and suppresses the inferiority complex. But other things seldom are equal, and in that case, Sympathy, Knowledge, and the Truth outweigh all that the mixed school can offer. (DuBois, 1935, pp. 334–335)

As W.E.B. DuBois challenged his peers in the 1930s to consider the profound and contradictory consequences of "mixed schools," so, today, the nation writhes in a moment of painful reflection on desegregation. Since 1960, public schools in the United States have become substantially less integrated by both race and class (Orfield, Easton, & The Harvard Project, 1996; see also Taylor, Piche, & Trent, 1997). The notion of K-12 integration has become passe, unrealistic, or undesirable for many. Instead, as Gary Orfield and colleagues

Chapter 5 previously appeared in *Construction Sites* (pp. 161–179), Lois Weis & Michelle Fine (Eds.), 2000, New York: Teachers College Press.

(1996) argue, too many communities are rushing toward neighborhood schools. DuBois is rapidly becoming a prophet into the 21st century.

Over the past few years, Denver, Seattle, Kansas City, Buffalo, Little Rock, and scores of other communities around the country have been released from their desegregation agreements. It was too hard, not effective, or not enforced. There may be few communities still willing to try to make real the dream of *Brown v. Board of Education* and Martin Luther King Jr.

So, too, national opinion shifts, retracted by race. A 1999 Public Agenda survey found that

> African American and white parents see great value in having their children attend integrated schools. About 8 in 10 black parents and 66% of white parents say it is very or somewhat important to them that *their own child's* school be racially integrated. . . . [But] despite widespread support for the concept, there is a distinctive lack of energy and passion for integration among both black and white parents. Only a slim majority of black parents (52%) say the nation should do more to integrate schools. It is even harder to detect an appetite among whites for invigorating integration efforts: Only 27% want the U.S. to do more. (p. 11; emphasis in original)

The ambivalence about K-12 integration is palatable. In higher education, the retreat from integration is far more explicitly mean-spirited. In the 1990s, public universities on both coasts began to lock their doors to poor and working-class students, especially students of color. In the West, California's public universities radically rolled back on affirmative action, substantially reducing the numbers of African-American, Latina/o, and Native-American applicants and students accepted. In the East, the trustees of the City University of New York have waged a battle to restrict open admissions and withdraw re-mediation at 4-year colleges, thereby denying educational access to thousands of poor and working-class students of all racial and ethnic groups (for evidence in support of affirmative action higher education, see Bowen & Bok, 1998). At this contentious moment in history, we write with the gall, the desire, and the sense of obligation to insist on public educational spaces that promise integration, offer democracy, and assure racial and class justice—before the bleach gets us all.

Over 2 years, we have had an opportunity, generously supported by the Spencer and Carnegie Foundations, to collaborate on a study of high school detracking in northern New Jersey, the fourth most segregated state in the nation. This is a district in which students, primarily Whites and Blacks, range from extremely poor to extremely wealthy; a district in which all schools are "integrated" by court order, but where the high school tracking system of high honors, honors, and regular tends to resegregate. High school students across race and across social-class lines rarely mingle during their academic periods.

Montclair, New Jersey, is one of the few communities nationwide that has worked to keep the dream of integration alive, not without troubles, not without disappointments, not without a court order. But the town has struggled to provide both excellent and equitable education to all its students—poor, working class, middle class, and rich; White, African American, biracial, Latino, Asian American.

In this high school, in 1993, educators took it upon themselves to challenge the school's (and district's) structure of tracking. Educators in the English Department, inspired (and then chaired) by Bernadette Anand, argued that ninth grade English be detracked for all students, offered at the level of high honors (for a review of tracking research, see Oakes, Wells, Yonezawa, & Ray, 1997). A world literatures course, with high standards for all, would be taken by all.

Predictably, as Wells and Serna (1996) have written, the town blew up and, as predictably, it eventually settled down (for a history, see Fine, Weis, & Powell, 1997; Karp, 1993; Manners, 1998). Since that time, the current mayor has run on a platform to do away with the course, on which the school board is deeply split. Some Whites protested publicly that their children's chances of admission to Ivy League colleges would be jeopardized, and a number pulled their children out of the public schools. A small subset of the Black and White middle-class/elite families were concerned but remained publicly quiet. Yet a powerful multiracial and cross-class coalition of educators, parents, and community activists organized and prevailed. The ninth grade world literatures course has celebrated its 5th birthday in 1998. Still treated officially like a family secret, many in the community recognize it as a family jewel ("No Racism Found in Teaneck Schools," 1998).

With this brief history, we now wander into this course to understand how a space for youth can be designed within a public school both to produce "smarts" in all and to model racial/class democracy. Drawing on 2 years of Michelle's participant observation (2 days per week, sitting in on five classes per day) and more than 50 years of combined public education experience for Bernadette, Carlton, and Dana, we write this chapter from our very different standpoints. For 2 years, Michelle observed a series of ninth grade world literature classes that embody the best of this town. In this course, students reading on a third grade level converse, write, argue, and finish projects with students who have been reading the likes of Morrison, Whitman, Homer, and Cisneros since they were quite young. In this class, the chasms of race and, more precisely, of class are bridged by the talent of educators, the rigor of the curriculum, and the elasticity of youth. Everyone has been reading *Of Mice and Men* (Steinbeck, 1937), the *Gilgamesh* epic (1992), *Nectar in a Sieve* (Markandaya, 1954), *Antigone* (Sophocles, 1984), and *Two Old Women* (Wallis, 1994). Everyone is writing critical essays, literary reviews, creative works, and character analyses. Students who have been educated, to date, within relatively segregated gifted classes are hearing voices they had never before heard. Students who had been in segregated special education classes are learning they have things to say, poetry to write, critical analyses that deserve public audience. The choreography of the teaching is breathtaking—and exhausting.

On Monday and Friday mornings, in chairs too hard for my aging body, I (Michelle) am the delighted, intellectual voyeur to this work of integrated education. High-quality courses, rigorous standards, and heterogeneous groups of students engage together to produce new forms of knowledge, discovering how narrowly we have circumscribed what counts as "smart," inviting buried treasures to speak, creating at once a community of intellectuals and citizens.

But this work has a price tag. To educate all thoroughly, efficiently, and in sprawling multiracial communities means that a community must take seriously the costs of busing, early education, multicultural curriculum, professional development for teachers, even summer courses for those who are falling behind. The price will not be extravagant, but high-quality education costs.

Throughout this chapter, we reflect critically on two years' worth of data, and present the patterns of two cohorts of students, each moving through the course of one year. We consider how a space within public school, marked by race and class integration, stretches to create an intellectually engaging context for all. At one and the same time, these three teachers work to inspire and support those students who enter the course biographically assured of their (assumed natural) academic advantages *and* those students who have long been convinced of their (assumed natural) *in*ability to work through challenging texts. While inviting new voices to speak, they also insist on an ethic of respectful listening. This is a space that constructs what Jana Sawicki (1991) calls "radical pluralism," that enables a re-vision of social possibilities for and by youth. We trace the bumpy road of this space—contradiction-filled, if thoroughly integrated—recognizing how increasingly rare such spaces are today in U.S. public schools. Drawn from Michelle's participant observation and grounded in interactions in and beyond Carlton's and Dana's classrooms, we collectively write a biography of a public space for intentional interruption, a space for rigorous democracy, grown among youth and adults across "differences."

The text carries the powerful legacy of Bernadette Anand, evident in her words throughout, as we examine classrooms constructed by Carlton and Dana. No longer at the high school, Bernadette is the principal of a highly respected, very rigorous, extremely diverse middle school in Montclair. In this story, we are self-conscious that the text moves across an academic year as if September through June represented a "true" line of progress. Instead, as any educator will attest, a school year is punctuated by loops, surprises, backslides, and rewinds. September to June does, however, capture a flow of the class, a set of collective moves over time. Indeed, some incidents and relations that happen in June could not have occurred in September.

I (Michelle) delight in this narrative journey because these three educators have enabled and invited us all to look closely at a space in which racial, gendered, and economic power are self-consciously analyzed and interrupted; a space in which re-vision is insisted upon; a space orchestrated and negotiated by educators who dare to challenge *The Bell Curve* (Hernstein and Murray, 1996), refuse to hide behind the illusion of "neutrality," demand high standards for all, and well up with tears when most students rise to the occasion.

The educational project cultivated here necessitates that educators and youth create a space of intentional interruption in which young people can think through world literature and the complex relations of class, race, gender, and sexuality around the globe. This is a space in which all ninth graders are included: those delighted, those appalled, and those terrified.

A space in which youth, across race and class, engage with vigor will never occur by chance, by accident, or without leadership. Nor will it be applauded by our colleagues, supervisors, parents, or students in unison. And yet, we assume in this chapter, and in our work, that this is precisely our public responsibility—to create just such classrooms for and with youth.

SEPTEMBER–NOVEMBER: THE VICTIM-BLAMING MANTRA

With texts, students, anxieties, memories, colleagues, budget crises, faculty cuts, and wild anticipation, the year opens. It's September and we bend the spines of new books, launch new lives, try novel identities, and sneak toward new relationships among these 14- and 15-year-old bodies filled with delight, dread, hormones, excitement, premature boredom. For some, the room is filled with friends. For all, the room is also filled with strangers.

Today, they're discussing *Of Mice and Men* (Steinbeck, 1937), in particular George and Lennie's relationship at the end of the book. Carlton Jordan asks his students to form what he calls a value line: "Stand on my right if you think it was right for George to kill Lennie. Stand on my left if you don't. Stand in the middle if you are of both minds."

Much to my (Michelle's) surprise (and dismay?), the room tips to the right. The crowd moves in those loud clumsy teenage feet over toward the "it's OK to kill" side. I look for patterns by gender, race. Nothing. To the left wander three boys, a bit surprised and embarrassed, two White and one Black, feeling like they are going to lose. "But it's never OK to kill a friend," insists Joshua.

Carlton, momentarily stunned but never stumped by his "pedagogical failure" to get equally distributed groups, undermining his "plan" to set up pairs to discuss their positions, invites them to sit in groups and discuss.

The "it's OK to kill a friend" group gets loud, animated, vile. "Lennie's stupid." "He's the biggest retard in the world. He likes to pet dead rabbits. He don't need to live," shouts Kizzy—Muslim, brass, wonderful, noisy, always the voice that provokes Darren, an African-American boy, to respond with emotion. Sofia continues, "He should have killed Lennie long ago; he's a burden." Kizzy continues: "He's stupid. He murdered cold-blooded. We got to make him bad if we're gonna get George off." Eli joins, "By killing him, it was like saving a life."

Carlton and I exchange glances. I'm thrown by the raw but vicious analyses of these young adolescents and their endless creativity. The screams of "stupid, useless, dumb" are rusting my soul.

Carlton is as visibly shaken as I am. A strong, bold African-American educator, he begins to teach, to preach, to speak with his heart, his eyes, his arms, and his mouth. "Let me say something about Lennie, because, as I walk around, I am disturbed. What are the characteristics of Lennie?"

The class volunteers: "Stupid, slow, dumb!"

Carlton continues. "Dumb. Retarded. When you use language like that, I have to speak. You may say it was right for George to kill Lennie because Lennie killed someone else or Lennie would have been killed. There are many reasons. But because [he] is stupid, slow, no. Some of you have learning disabilities. Some of you have persons with autism or retardation in your family. And none of us knows what's coming next. It is important to see Lennie as a man, as a human being, not as something that should be destroyed."

Kizzy: "But he stupid. You are coming down on our group."

My mind wanders. Remembering the calls [from some White parents] to the superintendent about "them," remembering talk at the school board about how "those students" will hold back "the motivated ones," I am brought back to the room by Carlton's voice. "Some of you have been called stupid by others. You have to think about what it's like to be in a world where everyone seems to be getting it right, and you don't even know what you don't know. Some of you sit in lunchroom and won't eat tuna sandwiches because you're going to save the dolphins, but you'd laugh at Lennie in our school. Some of you will send money to Rwanda and Bosnia to save children over there. But you would make fun of Lennie, throw stones or shun Lennie over here." The students have reproduced the discourse being narrated about them. "George should not be burdened by Lennie." That is just what some at the school board meeting were implying.

Carlton: "Let me say, I take this personally. If you can't walk with Lennie, if you can't see Lennie as a human, as a brother, what future is there for our community? What possibilities are there for us as a whole?"

Class is over. I'm feeling exhausted and depleted, and amazed at the strength of a teacher willing to speak, interrupt, listen, and educate. After a weekend of worries and exchanged phone messages with Carlton, I returned to class on Monday to re-find "community," orchestrated by Carlton, already at play.

The lecture opens with a discussion of first-person and third-person narratives. Carlton asks students to "turn to a page of *Of Mice and Men* where George and Lennie are interacting. I want you to rewrite the passage as Lennie. In first person narrative. To see how Lennie's wheels turn."

"What wheels?" snipes Paul.

The students clip through the text, muttering, but writing eagerly. Carlton waits patiently for volunteers. Hands shoot up. "I am just a happy man, likin' my rabbits." "Why George callin' me a stupid so and so." Hands of all hues fill the air. The room is alive with Lennies.

"How do you feel?" asks Carlton. "Stupid?" The point was made. Carlton was crafting a community not yet owned by students, but the students were growing extensions with which to connect in the room and beyond.

A parallel exchange occurs in Dana's classroom, early in October. Note how powerfully the character of George is relentlessly protected by the students, while Lennie is ruthlessly discarded as if disposable.

Charles: George is trying and Lennie is holding him back.

Erika: Lennie died happily. George did what he had to do. He gave a final request about rabbits. It's not right to kill, though.

Ben: It's not George's fault.

Dana: Why not?

Ben: If he had known what Lennie was thinking, maybe. But George is off the hook.

Dana: Who is solely responsible for ending the life of Lennie?

Angela: I still feel exactly the way I did before what you said. Lennie couldn't live.

*   *   *

Shana: George wanted Lennie to die. It's not fair for Lennie. Maybe George, in the back of his mind, Lennie was such a burden.

Mikel: I'm not sure, Curley was going to do something. George
protected himself.
Liza: Lennie is a nothing. He's a sausage!
Dana: Is it hard to hang out from Lennie's point of view?
[Dana and Carlton insist, but don't yet prevail. The students in
September and October refuse to view social relations from
the bottom.]

Across the five classes, we hear a ringing, shared, often painfully
victim-blaming consensus—in September and October—in which
most *who speak* agree that Lennie is a "loser," a "leech," a "sausage,"
and that social relations are inherently and fundamentally hierarchical,
competitive, and back-biting. These are the Reagan-Bush and now
Clinton children of the 1990s. These are the children who have been
raised on policies that are anti-immigrant, antiwelfare, anti–public
sector, pro-death penalty, anti–affirmative action, "national/mater-
nal" ideological milk. And many seemingly swallowed. If I (Michelle)
were to report on only what I heard from September through November, the Right could relax. These preadolescent youths have been
well trained by a nation armed with victim-blaming rhetoric. In the
beginning of the year, while there are pockets of silence and some
raised eyebrows, moments of "Wait a minute . . . ," we hear mostly
that "murder and crime can keep the population down," that George
was "entitled" and Lennie "dispensable." And so, too, we witness
fatigued teachers, still standing in the front of the room, trying to
create a space that provides a view from the bottom, a moment of
empathy, a peek from another angle. In the interim, victim-blaming
analyses, a longstanding tradition in the United States—in a kind of
White and Black hegemony—can be (and were) a horror to progressive
educators standing in front or sitting in the back of the room. Yet
in this class, over time, many students are encouraged to produce
kaleidoscopic understandings of social issues, to engage standpoints
that are shifting, and to reject victim blaming.

By mid-October, having finished *Of Mice and Men* (Steinbeck,
1937), Dana's class has moved on to *Two Old Women* by Velma Wallis
(1994), a Native-American woman from Alaska who retells a story
told to her by her mother. The story tells the tale of two old women
left to die, abandoned by their community.

Dana: In the book *Two Old Women*, where two Alaskan women
     are left to die by their tribes, should the two old women
     have forgiven the tribe?

Ben: Maybe they should. It was their time to go. It was their
     survival.

Dana: I heard that for George [protection of the power-
     ful].

Michael: I don't think they should forgive because they weren't
     helpless or lame. Just old. It wasn't right. They shouldn't
     forgive.

Angela: I was raised to believe old are wiser and keep heritage
     alive. From old you get new experiences, but young have
     little to offer. Even though they were old they were strong-
     est in the book. Like Lennie.

Ben: If they didn't forgive, they couldn't last long. If we saved
     all old, we'd be overpopulated. Murder and crime may
     keep this earth's population in balance.

Dana: Do we bear *no responsibility* in the taking care of?

In the beginning of the school year, there are typically few who
will publicly annotate a perspective from the bottom. And yet, by
November students like Michael [Black boy] and Angela [White girl]
are beginning to chance another point of view, beginning to notice
that something is different. Their teacher is not simply a carrier of
dominant views, reinforcing only the view from above. Dana and
Carlton are offering many lines of vision and insisting that challenging
whispers get a hearing when they are voiced.

It is toward the end of this season of victim-blaming chill, when
parental calls to the superintendent start to come in, demanding to
know why Candace didn't get an A on the first draft, why Dana is
"bending over backward for *some* students," why Carlton is having
"political" and not "literary" discussions. These are the days when
"everyone has a choice" is declared as truth by some students, when
victims are blamed and those who challenge social arrangements
grow suspect—students and teachers alike. But work is yet to be done.
And at this point in the class, all students suspect that something is
up. The dominant conversation prevails, but on its last legs for this
year.

DECEMBER–FEBRUARY: THE MELTING, AND THEN PARTIAL RESTORATION, OF PRIVILEGE

Creating an intentionally interruptive space that is also safe for all means breaking down the invisible walls that segregate those historically privileged from those historically silenced, that separate traditionally "smart" from traditionally "slow," that challenge the categories and "right" answers that worked so well in the past. Forcing students to "come out" from behind their performances of nerd, athlete, scholar, clown, or dummy, we invite them to reveal and develop deeper, more complex performances of themselves. We model, chance, and push the very categories that they (and we) have taken for granted—categories that have celebrated some while suffocating others. And then, at moments in our classrooms, our attempts at social justice step right on the toes of academic traditions. Ruptures occur. Breaks and fractures explode. Crises boil over. Conflicts erupt. That's when we know we have done our work and that the most serious work of education is ahead of us.

Alas, by December, it is clear that the teachers invest in what might be called standpoint theory, an understanding that people think, feel, see, express, resist, comply, and are silent in accordance with their social power and that a view from the "bottom" may diverge dramatically, critically, and brilliantly from a view from the "top."

Even if a view from the "top" has been the standard, accepted as "best," assured an A+ to date, those standards, oddly, are no longer operating. Equally rigorous, new standards are emerging. We turn now to a discussion of the book *Nectar in a Sieve* (Markandaya, 1954), an analysis of dharma, fate, and hope, to notice the early awkward stages of trying to get all voices heard, without privileging elite or dominant perspectives that have long passed as the only form of "smart."

> *Seri (mixed-race boy):* People *live* based on hope.
> *Alison (White girl):* I think that's *sad*. If it's just based on hope, you need to study.
> *Pam (White girl):* You need not just *hope* but *goals*.
> *Cecil (Black boy):* My *hopes* are to do the best that I can, be a musician and NBA player.

Danielle (White girl): I think it's true. Everybody has *one dream* and they have to accomplish the dream.

Carlton: What keeps you in school?

Chris (White boy): I think about school, it's the future. College and further, career, family, and support.

James (White boy): Work hard.

Sara (White girl): My *goals* are based on education, not McDonald's.

Cecil: I would rather have McDonald's.

Sara (White girl): I don't want to *depend* on a husband or taxpayers or my parents.

Alison: Most people only have *hope*. That's sad.

Kareem (Black boy): Animals don't have hope, only people. Animals have instinct.

MF [Fieldnotes]: It's polarizing: Blacks defend hope and Whites defend ambition/goals as if hope were silly, as if this dichotomy made sense!

Hannah (White girl): Lennie doesn't know what hope means but he hopes to be as smart as George.

Qwuinette (Black girl): He does have hope.

Alison: Maybe ignorant people have more hope and smarter people are more cynical.

Cecil: You've got to be kidding!

Cecil carries the momentum here. The room spins, the conversation stops and then begins again, changed. These critical turns, upon which our pedagogy relies, are as necessary as they are unpredictable. We yearn to understand how we can nurture, cultivate, fertilize our rooms so that critical turns get a voice—and eventually get a hearing.

At this point, "smarts" are popping out of unsuspected mouths, bodies buried into oversized jackets. At the same time, perhaps in response, there is a parallel move, a polarizing performance. So, for instance, Blacks defend hope and Whites defend ambition/goal as though these were separable. As previously unheard voices sing, there is a subtle polarizing, a freezing of positions. Now that the voices are up, there is nothing automatic about creating a community of differences in this space.

It's becoming clear that student identities ranging from "smart" to "disengaged" to "at-risk" are unraveling—not so predictable. In integrated schools, as DuBois worried, sorting typically means that a small core of students, usually White and/or middle-class students, rise like cream to the top and blossom as institutional signifiers of merit, smarts, advanced achievement (Bowles & Gintis, 1976; Moore & Davenport, 1989; Ryan, 1971). It is their loss most profoundly dreaded by public education. Today urban and suburban school boards live in terror of losing White and middle-class students across races and do all they can to keep them—even if that means holding other students hostage (Kohn, 1997; Sapon-Shevin, 1994). And yet this splitting is, as Eve Sedgwick (1990) would argue, fundamentally parasitic. The structural splitting elevates one group while it *requires* that others (Blacks, working-class/poor, disabled students) be seen as lacking. Funneled through a lens of hierarchy and limited goods, standards, achievements, and excellence demand exclusivity. Michel Foucault (1977), Erika Apfelbaum (1979), and, most recently, Jean Anyon (1997) have argued in very different contexts that power is always in and around classrooms. No classroom is Teflon-resistant to the winds of racialized, gendered, classed, and homophobic elements in America. The splitting into "good students" and "remedial students," which characterizes high schools and is interrupted in this classroom, reveals the workings of power. The ethnographic work in this classroom renders visible how power and privilege are ruthlessly enacted in integrated classrooms, evident particularly when educators seek to interrupt racialized and classed hierarchies.

Power operates as a set of social relations both inside and beyond the room. Outside the room, power is assured by the watchful surveillance of a resistant mayor and some school board members who threaten to "shut down" the course for fear of White/middle-class exodus from the public school and by the few educators and colleagues annoyed that these teachers dare to educate all to high standards, trivializing their work as "frills—more politics than rigor."

Within the room, as new voices emerge, mostly heretofore unheard Black voices, a kind of polarizing occurs. Again a small group of White students may decide to sit together, to reinforce each other's points, synchronize eye rolls when a student of color speaks. In ironic similarity to the oft-repeated "Why do all the Black students sit together?" at this point in the semester, there is a consolidation of a White-resistant position—not all, just a few, but enough to chill the room. The days of listening to "them" are over. It's important to note

that most White and most Black students don't glacialize. But most
are at a loss for how to engage this conversation outside the polarities.

Then I have a frightening thought: Is it possible that Whites work
"optimally," that is, uninterrupted, when we *don't* have to discuss
race and ethnicity and that students of color can only be engaged and
most unburdened when race and ethnicity are squarely on the table?
(See Billig, 1995; Fraser, 1990.)

As Linda Powell (1997) argues, it seems likely that students of
color are "stuck" until "race" is discussed, while White students are
"stuck" once race is discussed. Teachers (or students) who speak
through race, ethnicity, and class in the curriculum get accused of
dwelling on race—again! And a few outspoken White parents "save"
the White students (through phone calls) from the conversation.

By January, midterm grades are in, and the old stratification system is not layered like it used to be—no longer a two-tiered White
and Black cake. Carlton and Dana have been reading aloud to the
class some of the writings of students who sound like poets, like
journalists, like creative writers. Sometimes a White kid raises an
embarrassed hand when Carlton asks "Whose paper is this?" As often
an African-American boy from the back of the room will lift a reluctant
finger, or an African-American girl will hide her giggle as she sashays
up to the front of the room to reclaim her text. This moment is one of
both racialized melting and desperate consolidation of racial privilege.
The contrast sails through the room. Stakes are growing clear, as the
educators are riding broncos of resistance. This is a crucial moment
in a space designed to interrupt, a moment in which many give up.
But listen and you'll hear that these educators are relentless—over
Starbucks—in their commitments to re-vision.

> *Bernadette:* When you publicly state to the community, when
> you're only one course in the sea of all the other courses,
> that you truly believe in multiculturalism, and then you
> make the literature, the part, the actual content to open up
> those issues and the students begin to see the connections.
> And I think, even if they don't at the beginning, all of a
> sudden the other voices that never got heard someplace
> down below, they may have had these people in the class-
> room with them, all of a sudden these voices come and
> somebody turns around and says, "Whoa!" And they'll say

that to you. They'll say, "I didn't know so-and-so was so smart." And then, someone else's voice is honored, is sort of affirmed through that one student, and through yours. And everybody starts, the classroom is never the same after that.

Dana: That's when the phone calls, that's when you start getting calls. When you start, when other voices start to be heard and the kids start to see that you're actually giving validity to other writers, and then they see that when certain kids, the kids who are always there at the center of the room, start to see that they're not any longer the center of the room, all of this subversive activity starts. And the challenging, the constant challenging of your ethics and of your teaching ability. . . .

Carlton: It's like a disability of privilege. What are they holding onto? But the only way they can make the connection is to co-opt it, that it has to become their hurricane. They have to define how the winds move and whether they go from north to south. If it's not mine, how do I conquer it? I know it better than everyone else and will make people listen to me. This is a problem of privilege that needs remediation in our course.

At this point, a small set of relatively well-off White students (not all, but a few in particular and in full voice) search to reclaim status by displaying their family treasures, what Pierre Bourdieu (1991) would call cultural capital: "My mother is a literary agent, and she said *Two Old Women* never would have been published if the author wasn't a Native woman." "Have you read any of Sigmund Freud? My father is a psychoanalyst, and he would contest your interpretation." "My mother is the chair of the board of ——— and she said that Camden is lucky that outsiders have invested money because there was *nothing* there before." Some, at this point, less decorated with biographic merit badges, simply assert that "Today, in this country, we *all* have choices." Oppression and history are deemed largely irrelevant. A few gracefully sneer or turn away when students of color talk about race (not again!). I (Michelle) time the conversations that address race: The average conversation lasts 30 seconds. The record conversation lasted 45 seconds before someone shifted to, "But I don't think it's race, it's class." "It's age." "What about Whites in basketball?" "What about sexism?" "How about when you say faggot?" "But the Holocaust was . . . " And we're off . . .

Old lines are being redrawn, gentrification in academic blood. A sharpened White line of demarcation is being drawn. Interestingly, most White students refuse to employ these displays or barricade themselves, but they don't know what else to do. They can't yet invent another discourse of Whiteness. And so they retreat to a kind of silence, sometimes wonder, sometimes embarrassment. A few seem delighted that those who have always "won" —from prekindergarten to eighth grade—are not the automatic victors in this class. Like a fight in a hockey game, it is part of the work—not an interruption and not a failure. Re-vision. There is more to learn on the other end of this struggle.

MARCH–APRIL: PLAYING WITH POWER, SHIFTING AND REVERSALS

It's been a long stretch, but some of those students who never expected to be seen as smart, never expected to get a hearing from teachers or peers, are now opening their mouths, challenging myths and stereotypes, rejecting lines of vision from the top represented as if "natural" or "what everyone believes." And these challenges are getting a hearing.

There is a long conversation about the story *The Legend of La Llorana*, by Rudolpho Anaya (1991), a literary giant of a text about Cortez and Malintzin, about the conquest of Mexico. In the final scene, Cortez is invited to return to his homeland in Spain. Cortez insists upon taking his sons to Spain, lest they become "savages" and "uncivilized." In response, Malintzin, their mother, a native unwilling (and uninvited) to go to Spain, ultimately kills the boys in the belief that their death will liberate the people of Mexico. Dana has invited the students to prepare a mock trial of Malintzin.

"Is she guilty for having killed her children?" The pros and cons polarize almost immediately. The most vocal White students form a chorus, "You should never kill your children." "She must have been crazy." The most vocal African-American students circle around another question, "What do you have to do in order to survive oppression?" Four Black boys refuse to take sides, "You never kill *and* it was a time of incredible oppression."

Aziz, an African-American boy, breaks the stalemate, reversing the power and insisting that the trial of Malintzin is itself contained within colonialism. He queries, "Why is Malintzin on trial? Why isn't the Captain [Cortez] on trial?" At once the air thins, the fog lifts, the fists of power are sitting in the center of the room. The debate is not about Malintzin's innocence or guilt but rather about who decides what is the crime—colonialism of a race or murder of two children? Now, three quarters of the way through the term, questions of power are engaged, often, but not always, by African-American males like Aziz.

The theater is alive. Girls, for the most part, are carrying on the debate about social injustice. Some African-American girls assert their position in a discourse of power and inequality. In response, some White girls displace a discourse of power with a discourse of psychology, motivation, and equal opportunity. Trying to be sympathetic and inclusive, they may offer up universals such as "everyone loves their children" or "we were all raised to try to achieve," while African-American girls, equally insistent, are more likely to draw attention to power, difference, and inequality. Typically an African-American girl is pressing a question of race, class, and gender alone, and yet she stands sturdy, bold, and alone, often without support in the room. The room coalesces around its desire for her just to stop. The end of the year is riddled with a series of power eruptions. The dominant hold is cracking and freeing everyone. Splinters fly.

MAY–JUNE: COALITIONS, STANDPOINTS, SPEAKING TRUTH TO POWER—PREPARING FOR THE "REAL WORLD "

This course is messy. Little can be said that is linear, developmental, moving forward in a predictable line. And yet, with strong pedagogical commitments and the reading of great literatures these educators invite young minds to travel, to tackle the perspective of others, to review their perspectives of self. In this context, there are sometimes fleeting and sometimes sustained moments of coming together across "differences."

Students stretch, as a collective, to cross borders of race, class, gender, and "difference" and meet each other in a June Jordan poem, mourning for Rukmani, angry at Cortez, reciting what Lennie in *Of Mice and Men* (Steinbeck, 1937) might have really been thinking. These moments of coming together are, for us, the hope, the point, the real metaphor for America as it could be. For in these moments of coming together, students and faculty embody their differences in a chorus of voices, in a tapestry of cloth, in a fruit stand of delicious points of view. Very smart and bold, not compromising, not "Whiting out" differences, not "not noticing" but standing together, even if for a moment, challenging the separations that we adults—the "other" America—try to impose on them. Coming together to build knowledge, community, and serious intellectual work through and across race, ethnicity, class, and gender.

From May through the end of the term, students have learned to engage in this space, for 45 minutes a day, with power, "differences," and a capacity to re-vision. Some with delight and some still disturbed. Everyone will get a chance to speak and be heard. They will be surprised, still, to learn that "*she* said something so smart" or "*he* plays golf?" By now (finally), it is no longer rare to hear White students refer to, grow a conversation off of, interrupt with praise, or even disagree with students of color, or to observe African-American students challenging, extending, or asking a question of a White student. These may sound like minor accomplishments, but in a sea of parallel lives stratified by geography, class, color, friends, language, dress, music, and structures of tracking around them, the moments of working together, not always friendly or easy but engaged across, are worth comment. For these are moments that, once strung together, weave a frayed tapestry of cross-racial/class practice inside and outside of schooling. It is at this point in the semester when students assert positions from a standpoint. And they shift. They may risk a statement that will get little support from peers; they may dare to not support a lifelong ally/neighbor/friend; they may wander into a more treacherous alliance with someone previously unknown; they may challenge a comment that sounds, on the face, racist or homophobic even if a Black person, or a White person, uttered it. They may opt for a coauthored poem, a joint extension project. It is in this moment that the tears of the ethnographer fall too easily, when after a protracted conversation about race and power, John, a young man I had "coded" as middle-class and Black, offered, "These conversations are very hard for me. I understand both points of view. You all think I'm Black, but actually my mom is White and I could take either position in the room. But I don't talk much because I don't think anyone will catch my back." His eyes fill with tears as do those of many others in the room. There is a stunning silence. "I just felt confused." At which point, from across the room, on the diagonal, Eddie has begun the pulse of clapping that waves across the 24 young men and women. The writing has changed, sometimes dramatically.

At this point in the year, the end, at the just-arrived-at point of fragile, transitory, fleeting cross-race and -class alliances, students "choose" what level of courses they will pursue in the tenth grade. This school is as hyperbolically organized as most integrated schools: The 3 tenth-grade tracks are high honors, honors, and regular. High honors is the level at which ninth-grade English is offered, doubling in tenth grade as Advanced Placement. Regular is the more remedial level of English.

One day in the spring, I was shadowing a young White ninth-grader, Zach. It was the day he had to "choose" the level for his tenth-grade social studies. He and two African-American ninth-grade male students opted for high honors. I noted to myself how unusual it was for two African-American boys, in this system, to self-select into high honors. The town is filled with scuttlebutt that "the reason so few African-Americans are in high honors is that they don't *choose*. Peer pressure, wanting to be with their friends, low self/teacher expectations keep them out." Now, the threesome approached the social studies teacher's desk and requested high honors. To my surprise, loud enough for us all to hear, the teacher responded, "High honors? You three are not mature enough to be in high honors. Honors will do."

Zach, humiliated, visibly hurt and shaken, began pounding desks and lockers, insisting he would call his parents and appeal the teacher's decision (all quite admissible in this "choice" system). I approached the two other young men, the African-American students, and explained that they, too, could appeal. I would be glad to call home and suggest that their mother, father, or guardian elect high honors. They both "independently" responded, "No, that's OK. I can be in honors. That will be fine." And therein lies the perverse consequences of tracking, the limits of a "space" designed to interrupt hierarchy. As Franz Fanon (1967) predicted, Zach, the White boy, will appeal with an appropriate sense of outrage and entitlement. And he will prevail.

The African-American boys didn't, couldn't, didn't believe it was worth it, didn't believe they deserved it. No matter what the interior dialogue, the micropolitics of race and class operate through the bodies, the minds, the resistances, the assumptions, and the resignations of youth.

On good days, I (Michelle) am simply thrilled with the possibilities released in this course, this classroom, the intellectual, political, and relational opportunities launched from within this space. On bad days, when state and local budgets are so obviously and grossly cut with the blades of racism and classism, I despair. I despair that this course is a simple wrinkle in an otherwise fundamentally stratified national school system. Those with too much privilege fear so much their loss of privilege. And those with so little privilege are too delighted to not be in Newark. I despair that this course is not a free space at all, but an illusion of democratic access and engagement within a sedimented racial hierarchy, a number-by-color meritocracy, a cosmetic fissure in an otherwise fixed race/class formation. On really bad days, I worry it may be a con for students, a ploy, a tease, a contradiction. And at these moments, over something stronger than coffee, I turn to my colleagues, and we remember the power of the space in freeing an imagination for racial justice. We yearn for more such spaces but also recognize the power of the interruption. While we shiver over the ruthless onward march of systemic racism, we find comfort in the fissure within hierarchy and the gift these teachers have shared in this space with their students. We end this essay as we often end our coffee-based professional development, with the teachings of Maxine Greene (1995):

> We all learn to become human, as is well known, within a community of some kind or by means of some kind of social medium. The more fully engaged we are, the more we can look through others' eyes, the more richly individual we become. The activities that compose learning not only engage us in our own quests for answers and for meanings; they also serve to initiate us into the communities of scholarship and (if our perspectives widen sufficiently) into the human community, in its largest and richest sense. (p. 3)

Learning to Speak Out in an Abstinence-Based Sex Education Group: Gender and Race Work in an Urban Magnet School

LOIS WEIS WITH DORIS CARBONELL-MEDINA, ESQ.

> *Lois*: Oh, Donna [a young woman in the group] was say-
> ing . . . looking at a sheet that you had given them, you
> know, instead of having sex, you go for a bike ride, watch
> television, et cetera, et cetera. And Donna looked at the
> sheet and said, "Well, we can't do these things. We're
> poor. We don't have bikes . . . We don't have a car." And
> you [Doris, the group leader] turned to her, and, without
> missing a beat, said, "Well, you're going to be even poorer
> if you have a baby or get AIDS."

Recent research on sexuality education in schools suggests that
the current state of affairs is dismal. From Michelle Fine's (1988) research on what she terms the missing "discourse of desire," to work by
Mariamne Whatley (1991), and, more recently, Bonnie Nelson Trudell
(1993), we learn that in these curricula young men are painted as
biologically programmed sexual aggressors, while women are scripted
as passive victims whose only subject position is that of *not* provoking
easily sexually aroused males. While it is generally acknowledged that

Chapter 6 previously appeared in the *Teachers College Record*, 1998 (pp. 621–650). Used
by permission of the *Teachers College Record*.

there is not nearly enough sexuality education in schools, that which does exist leaves much to be desired. In addition, research shows that compulsory heterosexuality is inscribed throughout the school curriculum, and most prominently, in sex education curriculum, where AIDS is often drawn as a disease solely of homosexuals (Friend, 1993).

The general picture penned by a recent survey of state sexuality education policies and programs is quite discouraging. As Brian Wilcox (1998) argues:

> While most states have developed sex education curricula or curricula guidelines, the curricula and guidelines are often minimal and inadequate. Gambrell and Haffner (1993) found that fewer than a third of these materials included reference to any sexual behaviors other than abstinence. Discussions of sexual behaviors, when included, tended to focus on negative consequences of sexual activity. Potentially controversial topics, such as sexual orientation, abortion, masturbation and shared sexual behavior, were rarely covered. Few states required those teaching sex education to have certification in a specific field or receive training in sex education (p. 8).

While the federal government has played a leadership role in the establishment of publicly supported family planning services for adolescent girls, it does not play a substantial role in the development of sexuality education programs. This is not unusual given the general lack of federal investment in curriculum development in the United States. This apparent lack of investment, however, is deceptive in the case of sex education programs. Again, as Wilcox (1998) notes,

> Conservative politicians have repeatedly raised the concern that federal family planning services condone adolescent sexual activity by making contraceptives available to teens. In 1981, Senate conservatives led an effort resulting in the passage of the Adolescent Family Life Act (AFLA, Title XX of the Public Health Service Act). The sponsors of the AFLA legislation argued that prevention efforts including information about contraceptive use sent a message to teens that sexual relations were acceptable or inevitable, thereby promoting sex outside of a marriage. As finally approved by Congress and signed by President Reagan, the Adolescent Family Life Act restricted prevention activities to those that promoted sexual abstinence as the sole means of preventing pregnancy

and exposure to sexually transmitted diseases (Mecklenburg & Thompson, 1983), prompting critics to dub it the "Chastity Act" (p. 11).

Since that time, millions of federal dollars have been expended to support "abstinence-only" sex education. After a period of controversy over the money and programming in the early 1990s (Wilcox, 1998), federal support for such programs is again increasing.

The Personal Responsibility and Work Opportunity Reconciliation Act of 1996 signed by President Clinton and otherwise known as "welfare reform," contains a provision that will provide $50 million in annual matching grants to states which have "abstinence-only" programs. Every state in the union has, as of now, applied for such funding. In fact, "over the next five years the federal government will spend more on abstinence education than it has on the Adolescent Family Life Act combined over the past twenty years" (Wilcox, 1998, p. 13). Given that an evaluation component is not mandated, the value of this investment will not be known for some years, if at all. Clearly, though, support for the increase in funds was spurred by legislators' concerns regarding apparent rates of sexual activity and nonmarital childbearing by adolescent girls (Wilcox, 1997).[1]

There has, to date, been some excellent research on issues of sexuality education in schools (Burdell, 1998; Emihovich, 1998; Fine, 1988; Musick, 1993; Trudell, 1993; Whatley, 1991). However, there has been little research concerning the effectiveness of one type of program versus another (Kirby, 1997; Wilcox, 1997) and even less research on the day-to-day delivery of those programs that do exist.[2] Clearly there is cause for concern if money is being poured into abstinence-only programs, given the paucity of research which suggests any kind of positive outcome at all (Kirby, 1997).

The fact remains, though, that millions of dollars are being poured currently into abstinence-only sex education programs in schools without any clear idea of outcomes. Currently, most sex education programs in schools are *abstinence based,* including the one examined here. While abstinence-based and abstinence-only may appear to be a minor language difference, there is, in fact, major difference in content. *Abstinence only* programs present abstinence as the only option for adolescents and offer no additional content such as contraceptive information for those adolescents who may not be abstinent. In addition, such programs often use fear tactics to make their points. *Abstinence-based* programs, on the other hand, describe most sexuality programs in schools and offer information about safer sex techniques and contraception in the event that adolescents do not "choose" abstinence.

In this chapter I investigate one such abstinence-based program as funded in a magnet arts school in a large northeastern city and suggest that the space carved out by this program for girls is being used to promote the deconstruction of taken-for-granted gender and race meanings.[3] In this space, teen women struggle to topple the lives that they feel will be theirs, under the careful guidance of a Latina group leader whom I observed and worked closely with. In this urban-based magnet arts school, abstinence-based programming (mainstream sexuality programming) is being used for some very progressive ends, ends that encourage young women across race/ethnicity to explore their own gendered subjectivities and, most of all, resist the violence and control that they feel lies ahead of them. Writing with deep respect for the work of Michelle Fine, Mariamne Whatley, Bonnie Nelson-Trudell, and others who have pointed out the difficulties with mainstream sexuality curriculum, I want to suggest here that such curriculum can potentially be used in more progressive ways and, in fact, offers a space for such use that abstinence-only curriculum surely will not. While there may be great problems with mainstream sexuality curriculum, it is important to focus upon the space that such curriculum *could* offer if opened up and used in a more progressive manner.

It must be clear from the beginning, though, that hegemonic definitions of heterosexuality were not questioned in the particular group studied. This group was aimed, unofficially, at helping young women to gain strength and control within the boundaries of heterosexual relationships. It did not, therefore, broach alternative sexual orientations.

MY BOTTOM LINE AT ARTS ACADEMY

Data were gathered during spring semester 1997 at "Arts Academy," a 5–12 magnet school geared toward the arts in Buffalo, New York. Students must be accepted into the school on the basis of an audition, either in dance, theater, music or visual arts, or radio and TV. The school draws broadly from the city of Buffalo, although many of the students reside in poor and/or working-class neighborhoods within a 10-minute ride of the school. The school is located just south of downtown Buffalo and, like all magnet schools in the city, as part of the desegregation plan, ostensibly acts as a magnet for White students to attend school in neighborhoods populated by people of color. The school is highly mixed racially and ethnically, having 45% White, 45% African American, 8% Latino/Latina, 1% Native American, 1% Asian students. The ethnic/racial montage is everywhere visible, as students from varying backgrounds participate in academic and arts endeavors, spanning jazz combo to ballet.

Data were drawn from within a school program entitled My Bottom Line, a program whose officially stated goal is "to prevent or delay the onset of sexual activity, build self-esteem, and increase self sufficiency in young women through an abstinence-based, gender-specific prevention education program."[4] The program stresses abstinence as the preferred "choice," but does not steer totally clear of topics related to contraception and/or safer sex. Students voluntarily attend the program during study halls, participating one or two times a week, depending on the schedule. The guidance counselor actively recruited Womanfocus, a nonprofit agency designed to deliver the program to local area schools. It has the strong backing of the guidance counseling staff, and group meetings were held in the large, centrally located conference room of the guidance office.

As Shirley, the guidance counselor states,

> I really want these girls to take good risks with their lives and escape negative situations. I want them to be empowered to make good choices, to be able to leave town for college, to take internships, to take advantage of opportunities, to be able to leave their neighborhoods. Too many are trapped. I want them to delay sexual activity without being a prude so that they will be able to live fuller lives. Too many of these girls don't realistically see what a baby does to one's life. They have babies to make up for their own lost childhood and want to give to the baby what they themselves did not have. But they do not have the resources or maturity to give to their baby what they didn't have.

Shirley invited Womanfocus into the school, and used all school resources possible to support the program. She talked with teachers on a regular basis, urging them to send students during their study halls and worked with teachers to facilitate this.

My Bottom Line is run by Doris Carbonell-Medina, a Latina Womanfocus staff member. I participated in all meetings for a full semester and acted, at times, as cofacilitator of the group. The program ran 15 weeks. Although the program targeted young women in seventh, eighth, and ninth grades, young women from grades 7–12 participated, at the explicit request of Doris. Seventh and eighth graders meet together, and high school students meet in a different session.

The officially stated goal of the program is to reduce sexual activity among youth. As stated in the proposal for funding,

> The alarmingly high rate of teenage pregnancy, the risk of AIDS and other sexually transmitted diseases have served to open up and intensify the debate in this country and in the Buffalo community over what to do about the sexual activity of adolescents and the associated problems. What was once a moral issue is clearly a public health issue. Educators, parents, politicians, and health officials share concern and agree that clearly our current systems are failing to adequately equip our young people to handle the choices and the consequences they face in 1994.
>
> Current peer standards of sexual behavior, stronger media messages, shifting society values, and changing family configurations have all helped to confuse our teens as to how to handle their emerging sexuality. Abstinence, or refraining from sexual intercourse, has become a lost and understated option for many teens. At best, our teens are not getting balanced messages about their choices with regard to sexual activity. At worst, there is no evident, consistently reachable "face saving" support for the teens who want to abstain or delay the onset of sexual activity.
>
> Education for sexual abstinence, life skills to empower young women to assert their honest choices with regard to sexual activity, and the potential impact on adolescent sexual activity is the focus of the proposed My Bottom Line program (p. 3).

The expressed intention of the program is, then, one of encouraging abstinence among girls who are not yet sexually active; generally those in the seventh, eighth, and ninth grade. However, Doris insists on working with the older girls as well, specifically tying her decision to the rhetoric of abstinence:

Doris: Many people interpret abstinence-based program as, you know, very conservative, sort of right wing, concepts. Like that abstinence means they have to be "clamped shut," and you're saying, "that's it." And that's why we target those seventh-, eighth-, and ninth-grade girls, because those are the years that they're going to be facing those crucial decisions in their life, as to whether or not they want to be having sex. And those are the years that girls choose this for their lives. But, on the other hand, those high school girls that have already made that choice [to have sex], or some that haven't, they also need some sort of intervention, and that knowledge that simply because you've been sexually active in one relationship doesn't mean that you have to be sexually active in another relationship. And, you know, young girls need to be given that information, or at least to be given the confidence to say, "Hey, you don't have to sleep around with every single guy." There are some standards that you should have. There are some criteria that you should have in establishing your relationships. And I think those lines get blurred once you become sexually involved, and once you get into that whole world of adolescence and sex.

Tying her insistence on working with girls beyond ninth grade to a strongly held notion that these young women need to be given choices about relationships and sex even *after* they have had a sexual relationship, Doris works hard to let young women know that they do not have to be sexually available to every man simply because they are not virgins. In doing so, she stretches, intentionally, the purpose of the program:

Doris: You know, it's not that I don't care if they are having sex. If they are having sex, I just want them to be prepared to answer, if they are engaging in adult-like activity, that they should have adult-like responsibility. And that's where my focus is. Adult-like responsibility if you are, you know, assuming this way of life. And, I think that they need the confidence to know that they don't have to have sex with every guy that they go out with.

Lois: What do you mean by adult-like responsibility? You say it
would be better if they didn't engage in sex, but if they engage in sex, then they have to, number one, you don't always have to have sex, but number two, you have to do so
in an adult-like way. Can you say a little bit about what
you mean by that?

Doris: Sure. Adult-like way, you have to be able to protect yourself from unwanted pregnancies, that you have to protect
yourself from STDs (sexually transmitted diseases) and
other related diseases. That you have to understand that
you're placing yourself in a very emotional and vulnerable
position when you begin to, you know, act, and you conduct yourself in your relationship with him, yeah. And
that, a lot of times there can be some positioning that goes
on [in the relationship; she is speaking of control], and
even some abuse. And, I mean, your growth, you might
think this [abuse] is normal, that it's okay for them [the
young women] to be treated badly, or to be controlled. So
that if, in fact, this is happening to you, then you have to
recognize that this [abuse] is not right. And you have to
take responsibility for yourself and get out. And tell somebody about this problem. So that's adult-like responsibility
if you have a relationship with a member of the opposite
sex, particularly if he's older than you. But now, we're [in
the program] doing this thing that they're [the young
women] signing a contract [laughs]. . . . I devised this contract we outlined at the beginning of September. And we
talked about it, that the girls agreed not to have sex until
they can take care of themselves. And then I go on into it
and define "take care of yourself."

This space was, then, in addition to dealing primarily with issues
of sexual abstinence, intentionally established in order to empower
young women, particularly in their relationships with young men.
For Doris and Shirley, the guidance counselor who was the impetus
behind this program in the school, women's bodies must be under
the control of women themselves, and should not be a site for male
control, abuse, or exploitation. Both state strongly that women need
to evidence choices over their bodies and minds, and that the lack of

such choices means that these young girls/women will never venture outside their neighborhoods or their lived economic marginality. Empowering them to stay away from situations of abuse lies at the center of the unofficial programming. This is not, then, simply a program about abstinence, although the abstinence strain is there. Here, mainstream sexuality curricula are used as the bases for important discussions about gender, sexuality, and indirectly, race.

I, Lois, was not an evaluator of the program. I knew of the program since the coordinator of Womanfocus, Laura Myers, was my former Ph.D. student, and I knew that potentially interesting gender-based work was going on in this site. As part of a larger look at sites of hope in urban America, I wanted to focus specifically on a young women's site, one which was racially/ethnically diverse. As a piece of this larger look at what Michelle Fine and I refer to as "Urban Spaces" (Fine & Weis, 2000), I wished to focus on the ways in which the group potentially offers a space within which personal and collective identity work takes place and to assess the extent to which such a space offers a "home" within which social stereotypes are contested and new identities tried on. The question is posed here: What is the nature of the "gender work" going on in this space? And what are the implications for "race work" given that it is taking place in the particular context of the urban magnet school?

This project, as noted earlier, is conceived as part of a broader study of "urban spaces," and pushes theoretically the work of Sara Evans and Harry Boyte (1992), Nancy Fraser (1993), and others. Fraser argues that it is advantageous for "marginals" to create what she calls "counterpublics" where they may oppose stereotypes and assert novel interpretations of their own shifting identities, interests, and needs. She theorizes that these spaces are formed, ironically, out of the very exclusionary practices of the public sphere. We, too, have found that in the midst of disengagement by the public sector and relocation of private sector jobs "down South" or overseas, it is into newly constructed "free spaces," as Evans and Boyte (1992) call them, that poor and working-class men and women have fled from sites of historical/ pain and struggle, and reconstituted new identities (Fine & Weis, 1998).

In the broader study we stretch across spaces which are sites of explicit political resistance, such as those Boyte and Evans describe, to those that are more nearly recuperative spaces more aptly scripted by Oldenburg (1989). These are places for breathing, relaxing, sitting on a couch without the constant arrows of stereotypes and social hatred. Many of the spaces we have investigated, however, are spaces carved in conscious opposition by adults *for* adults (see Morton-Christmas, 1999, and Lombardo, 2000 for examples). Here we have a space set up as oppositional by adults *for* young women. In this space, which adults establish and facilitate, teens actively interact. Although the official intent of My Bottom Line is sexual abstinence, there is much other work going on in this site, both by adults and youth, which offer it as a powerful space for re-visioning gendered and race subjectivities as students gain a set of lenses and allies for doing social critique. As we have argued elsewhere, most youth have the potential for social critique, but this critique fizzles as they grow older (Fine, 1993; Fine & Weis, 1998; Weis & Fine, 1996). Here we focus on the preliminary consolidation of critique and enter the site, as I lived in it and worked with it, for 6 months. It is the gender and race work we visit here, work done under the explicit tutelage of Doris Carbonell-Medina, Esq.[5]

BARING SECRETS

A cornerstone of the group is confidentiality, a confidentiality which enables the girls to bear secrets without fear of recrimination or gossip. As Doris states,

> I tell them at the very beginning that this issue I take very seriously. And when we say that in order to build trusting relationships, in order to build relationships [in the group] where we can open up and tell our stories, that we have to be mature. And mature means that you don't go around and you gossip and stuff. Then I say that I get so crazy about this stuff that if it comes back to me that you've opened your mouth and blabbed—and that's how it's seen—you know, we'd ask you to leave. And that would be the way that we separate you from us, because we don't want you to be in our group if you can't keep our secrets. They're very careful about it I tell you. And they don't reveal anything [in group] that they don't want people to know. And then, if they've really got to get it out—and

many of them have done this to me—they have said, "Can I talk to you after the group?"

Embedded in the weaving of a new collective of young women across race lines is the bearing of secrets. The group is a space within which young women tell a great deal about their personal lives—the illnesses within their homes, the violence in their relationships, their fears spoken aloud when their "stepfather's moving back in with mom." Girls share secrets as they share strength and hope, jumping in to help each other with problems, sometimes life threatening, and other times, mundane. As they share secrets, they examine self and weave new identities, individual and collective. What is particularly striking in these data is the extent to which young White women reveal pieces of their lives normally not told. Although they are relatively quiet in group, as compared with African-American girls, for example, those who do open up contest the suffocating silence which envelops them. White women, whether adolescents or adults, are the most silent/silenced group with which we have worked (Weis & Fine, 1998; Weis, Maruszcka, & Fine, 1998), speaking softly about the horrors in their lives only in one-to-one interviews, never in a group context. But not so here. White girls are cracking that silence so typical of the group, sharing secrets in protected environments, working beyond the one-to-one encounters. They are hearing each other out as they unburden their problems. Girls from a variety of backgrounds unravel their stories within the group context. Listen to Tiffany, who speaks with Lois and Tia in group:

> *Tiffany*: I love my mother dearly. But, OK, she's manic depressive, but I love her dearly.
> *Lois*: Is she really manic depressive?
> *Tiffany*: Yeah, like she's got medication and everything. She's a manic depressive and my dad is schizophrenic—which is great for me [sarcastically]. . . . She doesn't make friends easily. I have to watch what I say, because I don't want to get her in a bad mood. She's on medication now. She's very caring, but she's smothering. Like, it's my birthday Monday, right. I'm like, since I was like nine, I have like, each birthday, I have a half an hour later that I can stay up. I mean, right now it's 9:30, and all my friends are sit-

ting there going to bed at 11:00. And on Monday, I get to
go to bed at 10:00 and that makes me so happy because I
can go to bed at ten [laughs].

Tiffany goes on to tell us that she went through a bout of clinically
diagnosed depression a couple of years ago.

Tiffany: Well, in the summer of the freshman year, two years
    ago, I like, it was like, well, the court thing, everybody's
    separate. They [my parents] go to court. And I have to
    choose who I want to stay with for this part of the summer
    and that part of the summer. And that's how I was just
    like, usually I'm all happy, you know, kind of like this [as
    she is now], kind of perky [laughs] . . . And so, like all of a
    sudden, I just . . . I remember sitting there on the bed and
    going, you know, "I can't do it anymore." Because I wasn't
    really happy. I was just getting tired. And I went into a
    slight, it wasn't a severe depression, but it was depression.
    I had medication and everything. And I just distanced my-
    self from it and I went to a doctor—a psychiatrist—and ev-
    erything, cause I like burst into tears at the slightest criti-
    cism.
Lois: Did they send you to a doctor?
Tiffany: Yeah, they sent me to a doctor. I went to a doctor be-
    cause I was losin' weight, because I weighed 108. And I'm
    five-foot eight. And I dropped like twenty pounds that
    summer. And my mom was really worried, because you
    could like see my ribs, and, you know, I was getting really
    thin and it was worrying her . . . I only got to see the doc-
    tor a couple of times. My mom pulled me out, I said [to
    the psychiatrist], "I'm going to see you a couple of times
    and then my mom's going to pull me out." She [psychia-
    trist] didn't believe me. I saw her a couple of times. My
    mom pulled me out. Because I knew it was going to
    happen, because they always do it. Where just, like, I
    didn't really like seeing her anyways because I didn't like
    to talk, and I figured I should have been able to figure it
    out by myself. I was fifteen and I was like, "I should have
    been able to figure out how to do it by myself."

Lois: But most adults couldn't, Tiffany.

Tiffany: I know, but that's just the way I felt, and still feel like
     that a little bit.

Tiffany speaks candidly about her clinically ill parents, weaving
through the discussion her own feelings as she attempts to live in her
mother's house. She is not the only one who speaks so openly about
home-based problems, and the uniqueness of this, particularly among
White girls, should not be underestimated. My Bottom Line offers a
space within which such secrets can be shared. Tiffany, of course,
does not receive professional help in a group of this sort. What she
does receive is support and understanding from her peers, monitored
by an adult who is sensitive to these issues. In addition, and perhaps
most importantly, someone like Tiffany feels less alone with her problems since she has shared them and learned, oftentimes, that she is
not the only one with such problems. While teenagers, to be sure,
often complain about their parents, this should not be seen simply as
a "gripe session." Tiffany's parents are ill, and the sharing of this
information, like the sharing of incidents of domestic violence, of
violence in a personal relationship, represents one step toward acknowledging the problem and obtaining long-term help. Doris meets
regularly with the girls outside the group, and urges them, in a more
confidential context, to seek additional help.

Within this same context, at another session, Connie (White) talks
about her parents' chronic drinking and her own fears about possibly
drinking too much. We urged her, within group, to pursue Al-Anon,
a support group for families of alcoholics, within which she can begin
to sort out the effects her parents' drinking have had upon her, and,
at the same time, concentrate on her own health. Sharing in this sense,
can be turned into direct action.

DISTANCING

Able to bare secrets, young women use the space of My Bottom Line
to fashion and re-fashion individual and collective identities. Under
Doris's expert guidance, it is a space within which selves are tried on,
experimented with, accepted, and rejected. A key piece of this identity
work among participants involves distancing self from those perceived

as "not like us." In this space, in this time, they pull away from others. Unlike previous work, however, which suggests that this form of identity work in urban schools takes place largely along we/they racial lines (Bertram, Marusza, Fine, & Weis, 2000; Fine & Weis, 1998; Fine, Weis, & Powell, 1997; Weis, 1990), particularly among working-class Whites, and most particularly boys and men, the particular form this distancing work takes here is that of distancing from other neighborhood youth and, more broadly, from other girls/women thought to be heading down the wrong path. Virtually all of the girls, irrespective of race/ethnicity, who attend group use the space to distance themselves explicitly from those they perceive to be "other" than themselves; those who will not make it, those who will end up pregnant at an early age, those who will be beaten at the hands of men. This is not an idyllic presentation of cross-race interactions and friendships, but rather reflects the observation that when "difference" is constructed in group, it is not constructed along racial lines. Girls from all communities articulate carefully that they wish to be different from those in their neighborhoods, those whom they leave behind in their pursuit of schooling and success. While this may not translate into intimate friendships across racial/ethnic lines, it does mean that the racial "other" is not constructed as the "fall guy" for any of the groups under consideration, contrasting sharply with Julia Marusza's data on girls in a White lower-class community center (1998). For none of the groups under consideration are the racial borders specifically erected against which one's own identity is then elaborated. Rather, identity is elaborated *across* racial and ethnic group as girls distance self from the "other," whether male or female, who will not make it. Certainly there is much racial identity work going on in other sites that reaffirms Whiteness, for example, in opposition to Blackness, much as previous work suggests (Bertram et. al. 2000; Weis, Proweller, & Centrié, 1997). However, in this site alternative positionalities are developed.

Witness Connie and Ayisha below, Connie, a White girl of modest means who lives in one of the racial borderlands of Buffalo, a place which is formerly Italian but now largely Puerto Rican and African American. Although Connie draws an "other," this "other" is racially like self:

> *Connie*: We live in a really small house. I don't have the things my friends have, like all of them at this school are having big graduation parties; I asked my mom to get some small

invitations from Party City so that we could at least have the family over; she hasn't even done that. I guess I won't have any celebration. All my friends are having these really big parties. They all have much more money than we do. We live in a really small house; I have a really small bedroom. My one sister lives with us with [her] two kids; another sister lives in a house owned by my father on 14th street. All my sisters are on welfare. We have been on welfare when my father wasn't driving truck. When he lost his job, we didn't even have food in the house. I would go over to my boyfriend's house to eat. His parents are real nice to me. I have no friends in the neighborhood. All I know is that I don't want to be like my sisters and my mother. Their lives have gone nowhere. I don't want to be like them. I want to have lots of money—and food. I want to go to college [she is currently attending the community college].

Connie continues: My dad is an alcoholic. He drinks all the time. One time he grabbed my mom's face and held it really hard. He really gets out of control when he drinks. I don't let him put me down though—I just tell him off.

Connie spends much time in the group discussing her own emotional/physical distancing from her alcoholic father, her immediate family, and neighborhood. The group offers a "safe space" in which she can air these problems and receive support for remaining emotionally separate from her family, for not being dragged down. At the moment, her boyfriend also offers this "safe space." He is 23; they are engaged, having met 3 years ago. The group supports this couple, although concerned that Connie might fall into a pattern of drinking like her father. Doris and the other group members check to make certain that Arturo (her boyfriend) is not abusing her physically. Unlike other White girls and women whom we have interviewed extensively, Connie and other group members talk relatively freely about family histories of alcoholism and physical and/or sexual abuse, thus engaging in a language through which one's own and others' circumstances can be understood. In putting this language on the table, they bury such histories far less often than previous research suggests (Weis, Fine, Bertram, Proweller, & Maruzsa, 1998). Additionally, in breaking the silence about alcoholism, welfare, and/or violence in the

White family, they shatter the myth that the White family has no problems, thereby encouraging young women across race/ethnicity to understand that such problems are indeed shared, as well as helping young women to face their own situations. Young women across race/ethnicity share their stories of pain and hope in group; the group becomes a space within which this dialogue takes place.

Ayisha, an African-American young woman of 16 who has a one-year-old daughter, also sees her task as one of distancing herself from the neighborhood in which she grew up. This distancing is nuanced, however, since she is entirely dependent on her family, boyfriend, and her boyfriend's family, in order to raise her daughter. She walks a fine line—needing to distance from those who will hold her back, but simultaneously recognize and respect those who help her move forward. All live in the same neighborhood:

> *Ayisha*: (discussing the neighborhood) Actually there is a small percent who are going to do something with their lives. I hate to see 'em like that, but it's like they're all going to go off, smoke weed and drink, go to parties, and hang around the fellows. You know, my mother always told me, "It's not ladylike to sit there and drink on the corner." It's just . . . I mean, they just don't care about their body. It's terrible to see. And I'll be trying to say, you know, I have some friends and they go do that. And I'll be like "You all shouldn't do that." "Well, just because you don't do it . . ." "OK. Whatever. Whatever you decide to do, I'm behind you. If that's what you're doing, OK, that's what you're going to do." But they're always calling me a preacher or something, you know, every time I try to talk to them.

Ayisha has a somewhat contradictory relationship with her neighborhood. She is supportive of others and understands that they are supportive of her. At the same time, she knows many are going down the wrong path,

> At the rate they're going, they're either going to wind up in jail or dead, because they're always into something; they're always doing something wrong, always. There's never a time that our neighborhood is peaceful, unless it's during the early morning.

... All this, it's like they'd be on the corner selling drugs, or some of them turn to using drugs. And I keep telling them, "That's not the life you want to live. But I mean, you have kids, you really have to think about what you are doing."

Many of these young women, particularly the African Americans, are very much connected to their families and neighborhoods, passionately caring about what happens in their communities, while at the same time drawing discursive boundaries around themselves which enable them to go to school and stay on the right track. They engage the "other" constantly, telling them that they are going down the wrong path, while at the same time setting them up as radically different from themselves. Mindy, a White girl living in a largely Polish neighborhood, expresses similar sentiments to Ayisha:

Mindy: Oh, the girls. I'm the oldest girl in my neighborhood by two years, and the youngest ones have just turned thirteen, no, they're going to be fourteen this summer. And all of them are pot heads and I try so hard, like, [to them] "You know, you're so young." And I feel like, I mean, I'm not that old either, but I've been through a lot of things that they're going through at that age. And I was like, I was like, you know, "I had sex at this age," and, you know, "I regret it," you know. And all this and that.
Lois: How old were you when you had sex?
Mindy: I was like fifteen and a half. I had just turned fifteen. And I told them, "I regret it." And even when I first had sex, I just didn't go out with this guy and have sex. I waited a while and I still told them, I was like, "I regretted it." You know, "you're going to regret it. Sooner or later, you're going to regret all these things that you're doing, and I'm just trying to help you." But they don't care. They'll just do what they want to do anyways. Like my ex-boyfriend's sister, she is getting a reputation of being a whore, and all this and that. And I tried tellin' her, "You know, Carla, you got to calm down a little bit." She is fifteen. And she messes with guys that are really like twenty-six, you know. And I said, "What does a twenty-six year old want to do with a fifteen year old?" And she said, "I

don't know, they really like me." I was like, "Get out of here!"

Mindy talks with the other girls in the neighborhood, trying to help them while at the same time using them as a foil against which what she sees as her own currently appropriate behavior is elaborated. While not denying that she did many of the same things at a younger age, she now weaves her femininity and sexuality differently, constructing herself explicitly in relation to others in her neighborhood. In Mindy's case, it is other *girls* who are centrally located in her discursive constructions. Others in the group focus on boys *and* girls in the neighborhood as they elaborate what they want themselves to look like in the present and the future. For some, though, like Mindy, it is specifically with the girl/woman subject that they are concerned.

This work of "othering" is done similarly across race and ethnic lines in the group, thus rewriting dominant race scripts of difference in poor areas (Fine & Weis, 1998) at one and the same time as they sculpt alternative forms of femininity/womanhood. All are concerned with elaborating a positive present and future for themselves and see themselves in relation to community "others"; those who do drugs, drink to excess, wear tight clothes, sleep with a lot of guys, walk the streets, don't take school seriously, see older men. The group provides an arena within which these actual constructions get worked through, between, and among participants. Witness, for example, the eighth-grade group below.

An Eighth Grade Group

Lois: OK, talk to me about the women in your community.
Krista: About ten-twenty they come out. [laughter]
Danielle: Just about every girl, like, on my street, had babies when they were about fourteen, fifteen . . .
Krista: And I know this one girl, she doesn't live on my street anymore, but she had a baby when she was like fourteen or fifteen, and she went back to the same guy and got pregnant again, so now she's got two kids. And I don't know a lot like that. But I know her, because I think she used to baby-sit me when I was little, but I don't know if he's there

and will come back to her, you know, better and everything. But she got pregnant again.

Lois: What about some of the other women?

Shantelle: Well, some of 'em is fast. They talk to the boys on the
corner. All boys on the corner is not bad. They wear a lot
of showy clothes.

Tonika: I was watching Jenny Jones, this twelve-year-old girl, she
wore so much makeup, she acts like she's about twenty-
three. And the makeup and stuff. All these girls had these
shirts like this [indicates very short], their chest sticking out.
I mean, all these short shorts, look like underwear.

Tish: My underwear is not going to be that short.

Tonika: I mean, they're wondering why they'd be getting raped
and stuff, even though it's [rape] wrong, but if you walk
out of there with your chest sticking out in some short
shorts, which is what they do, it's kind of like, what kind
of attention you're going to get? You think you're going to
get positive attention, you know?

Shantelle: OK. A lot of girls like have babies around my neighborhood. They don't have an education, so like they are
kind of, they're low educated, ain't got no money, broken
down house and everything, and they're talking to the people in the weed house and everything.

Gloria: The girls around my neighborhood, they all "Hos." And
they wear nasty outfits, and they go out with older guys.

Delores: They [older guys] just be using, they use you, and they
have like three other girlfriends, and they try to play it off.
When they get caught, they'd be trying to like, well, you
shouldn't have been doing all this, and all that stuff. And
they [the girls] can't do nothing about it.

The eighth-grade group, most of whom are African American at
this particular session, use the space to talk about "other" girls and
women in the neighborhood, carefully distancing themselves from
them, and asserting, through discussion, that they are different. By
publicly solidifying the boundaries of good behavior, they hope to
hang together and remain without problems.

This actual (and potential) discursive work takes place across
racial and ethnic groups. The fall guy is not a constructed racial other,

as is so common in urban (and suburban; see Kress, 1997) schools, but rather those neighborhood youth who are perceived to be headed down the wrong path. In the case of young women, it is those other girls and women, those who are fast, wild, wear tight clothes, who enact femininity and sexuality differently from what they feel is appropriate and safe, who provide the primary "other" against which their own individual and emerging collective self is created. While this may seem to mirror the good girl/bad girl distinction which is so deeply etched in male culture, and indeed it does in some ways, the fact is that these young women are working cross racially to live productive lives, lives which enable choices to be made and which are free from abuse. The young eighth graders know that the "older guys just be using them [these other girls]"; they have "three other girlfriends, and they try to play it off." When the guys are caught, they blame the young women for doing something wrong—"You shouldn't have been doing this and that." These 13-year-old girls understand this full well and use the group to talk about it. It is exactly this situation which they are trying to avoid, and they know that things only get worse as women grow older. They want to stay in school in order to assert some control over their lives, enabling them to make choices regarding sexuality, men, marriage, and a future devoid of physical and sexual abuse and harassment. While the officially stated goal of My Bottom Line is to encourage abstinence, much more is happening in this context; young women are weaving a form of collective strength that goes beyond individual abstinence—they are gaining a set of lenses through which to do social critique and opening up the possibility of cross-race political work in the future.

It is most interesting in this regard that while "race work" is not in the official curriculum of this project, it is done all the time. The distancing discussed above, which is a by-product of "baring secrets," encourages a form of gender collectivity that works across traditionally antagonistic race lines. Abstinence work, on the other hand, which is the official curriculum, is done some of the time, raising interesting questions as to what constitutes the lived curriculum as opposed to the intended curriculum of this or any other project. Curriculum theorists (Cornbleth, 1990; McNeil, 1986) have, of course, alerted us to the fact that what is distributed as curriculum in actual classrooms bears, at times, little resemblance to what is seen as the legitimate curriculum (that which is written). The same dynamic is at play here.

Doris intentionally stretches what is presented to these young women to begin with as she moves well beyond notions of abstinence in her own understanding of what these young ladies need.

> *Doris*: And so one of the things that I've learned is from
> Michael Carrera. And he's a well-known author in preven-
> tion, and he also serves as a consultant for programs all
> around the country. And one of the things that he stresses
> is that you just cannot help a youth with just one problem.
> You really have to approach the whole life of the youth in
> a comprehensive kind of way, so that you can't only talk to
> them about pregnancy prevention. You've got to talk to
> them about jobs and employment. And then you've got to
> talk to them about practical skills, like, you know, how to
> dress. I mean you have to be able to provide that for them.
> And then if they need educational assistance, you have to
> be able to provide a tutor for them. And you have to bring
> the family in because if you're not dealing with the whole
> family and you're just dealing with the young person, you
> know, it's not going to work. It's going to be, I mean, there
> are some families you won't be able to deal with, and then
> you have to be able to empower that youth, you know, to
> come into another living situation or what have you, be-
> cause it's not enough for the young people to just go to a
> community center and leave. I know realistically I can't do
> that at My Bottom Line because I don't have the resources
> and the facility to do that. But I can know about the infor-
> mation and say, "Okay I've got to link this child with oth-
> ers and to be able to find her a job. I need to be equipping
> her to be able to look presentable, speak well, and just all
> kinds of things that we take for granted, that young peo-
> ple, if nobody's telling them, how do they know? It's not
> just about preventing pregnancy.

The girls, too, stretch the project in that they interact with what is presented and create something new, in this case, a girls collectivity which works across race lines. By baring their secrets, they create a community, at least in this space at this time, which transcends individ-ual racial and even social class identities. It is the dialectic of lived

curriculum creation which is so noteworthy in this particular context—
the context of teaching about abstinence. We will see this even more
clearly in the next section.

CONTESTING SOCIAL STEREOTYPES

Spaces such as the one explored here can offer places where trite
social stereotypes are contested; where individuals and collectivities
challenge definitions and constructions perpetuated through media,
popular culture, and so forth. This is highly evident in this group, in
that the girls use the space, under the guidance of Doris, to challenge
taken-for-granted constructions of femininity, race, and teenagers in
general.

Doris's role here is important. She urges these young women not
to accept prevailing constructions of femininity and masculinity, and
to challenge race and gender scripts directly.

February 10, 1997: Field Notes

Doris and I were waiting for the girls to come in for group.
Just then Tia walked in for the fifth period meeting. Tia talked
about her former boyfriend who got a thirteen-year-old girl
pregnant and "now it is too late to do anything about it since it
is her fourth month." The girl lives two doors down from her.
Her mother's best friend is the mother of the young man involved, and that is how she found out. They had broken up already because she [Tia] had no time to see him, with school
and working at Wegmans, but she still cares for him. The boy,
as it turns out, is nineteen. Tia can't even look at the girl. She
considers her a "slut." She forgives the boy, because "she made
him do it," but not the girl.
Doris: "What do you mean you forgive the boy but not the
    girl?"
Tia: "But she *made* him do it!"
Doris: "She made him put his penis into her vagina? He had
    nothing to do with it at all?"
Tia admitted that he had *something* to do with it, finally, but
she still hates the girl since she is a "slut." Since the baby will

live only two doors from her, she will see the baby a lot, and she is angry about it. "How is she going to take care of a baby at only thirteen? She is a slut."

Working off of prevailing understandings that boys are not responsible for their sexual activity because they are hormonally programmed to want sex, unlike girls, whose job it is, therefore, to make sure that boys do not get aroused, Tia's response mirrors notions of sexuality and gender circulating in the broader society and available, as Fine (1988) and Whatley (1991) note, in sexuality curriculum. These understandings have it that if girls get in trouble, it is their fault, since they have the responsibility of ensuring that boys are not enticed by sex. This positions women as sexual victims of hormonally programmed males. Under this formulation, the only subject position for females is when they keep men from being aroused. Doris intentionally interrupts this set of understandings by posing the question, "She made him put his penis into her vagina? He had nothing to do with it at all?" Indeed, in the group, Doris, as leader, challenges the notion of victim in a variety of ways. While not specifically gender related, the following incident clarifies this:

May 4, 1997: Eighth Grade Group

We are doing a worksheet on setting long- and short-term goals.
Doris: Let's get down to the three things I want to improve in my life.
Charisse: Can I go? My grades, my attitude, my allowance.
Shandra: You should say my attitude three times. You got a bad attitude.
Doris: Now that you've identified these, what short-term goals can you set that will help you achieve these goals?
Lavonne: Study more [they all start complaining about teachers who give them bad grades].
Doris: We're bellyaching again, ladies. If I want to improve something, who controls whether I do it? If you want to get better grades, who controls that?
Kathy: I'm trying, but these teachers are dragging me down.
Doris: Here we go. Blaming other people. What can *we* do?

Below, Doris guides the girls into more specifically gendered understandings, offering them space to challenge deeply rooted notions.

April 22, 1997: Eighth Grade Group

Doris: Is it good to be friends before having a boyfriend/girl-friend relationship?

Delores: I think you should be friends first, then if it don't work out, you can still be friends.

Ayisha: That don't work.

Patrice: I hate it when you make friends with a boy and then he doesn't want to take you out because he think you like a little sister.

Tonika: I hate it, most of the guys are taken, conceited, or gay [all laugh].

Doris: How old are you? [she already knows how old they are]

Response: Thirteen, thirteen, etc.

Doris: Don't you have a long way to go?

Tonika: No.

Ayisha: This one guy likes me. Everywhere I go he right there. When I go to my friend Phalla's, he right there.

Doris: Why is that a problem?

Ayisha: Cuz I don't like him. I don't want him to be around me.

Doris: Is this a form of sexual harassment? We walk down the street and someone calls after us. Don't we want real romance? You meet and fall in love?

Tish: But then you find out he's married.

Patrice: He's married and he's got a girlfriend.

Delores: He's married, got a girlfriend, and got kids by both of them.

Doris: What do we do when someone is in an unhealthy relationship?

Tish: Try to help them out.

Patrice: Get a restraining order.

Tonika: Talk about violence! When my mom was pregnant, her boyfriend hit her.

Patrice: My mom got beat up, then she left.

Doris: Well, we all know that relationships are bad if there is physical abuse.

Doris offers, in the above, the language of sexual harassment and makes certain that the girls understand that violence in relationships should not be tolerated. While these are obviously complicated issues and suggest no easy solutions, it is key that these discussions are taking place in a public space, indeed a school, under the guidance of a trained adult, who is suggesting that women need to develop their own power in relationships and not passively accept notions that whatever happens to them is their fault. She is, through the group, encouraging the girls to reconstruct what it means to be a woman/girl, working against the grain, offering an alternative voice to the deafening victim mentality. Helping the girls establish their *bottom line*—a bottom line that recognizes that women ought not be victims, comes through loud and clear in the group interactions.

The young women further the reconstruction of gender within this site, contesting what they see as male surveillance of women's bodies:

Susan: I'm uncomfortable around guys.
Lois: Why?
Susan: Oh, I don't know. Like, I had my dress, you know, not low cut, because that's not the way I feel comfortable, it's just like guys are always thinking about sex, and it drives me crazy. Because you know, with these guys on my street, I'm like, if they say 'hi,' or I went over, and going to talk to them, and I realized through the whole conversation this guy is just like staring at my breasts, you know. And they were staring, and I was like, "OK, bye," and I left. He was just staring at my breasts. Was he looking for them to see if they were there? They're so small, or what? I was "Hello." I just kept on with the conversation and I was like, looking down, looking up. What, guys? They're driving me crazy.

Kathy also resents what she sees as the male gaze:

Kathy: It's hard. It's like, especially when what you believe if it's not like what everybody else is doing. It's like really hard to like keep your word to it. There's a lot of pressure

out there. It's hard to really go out without like guys looking at you or something like that. I mean, I get freaked out.
Like all the news about rape and everything. I get freaked
out wherever I see like a guy just standing on the corner. I
go out driving and I like lock all my doors when I see
some guy just standing there by himself. But I get scared.
I'm really scared.

Ayisha challenges the construction of teenagers in general, and
especially the ways in which the school stigmatized her when she
became pregnant:

Ayisha: It's hard because it's so . . . it's a lot of pressure on you.
It's like everybody's like, take me, I had a baby and everything, and everybody was like, you know, put you down
and tell you that you're not going to make it.
Lois: Who put you down?
Ayisha: It was like people in this school looked at you funny.
Like the administration, they really did like, "Hm, hm,
hm." All these young girls, they be like, "Well she's the
junior class vice president." I stay after school many days
and help out. I played "Hello Dolly" [she is a trumpet
player]. I did that when I was pregnant. I did "Gypsy," I'm
learning those plays and sitting there playing the trumpet
and they're looking at me like, "OK. She's really good." Because I really enjoy music, *and you're not going to put me
down because I made a mistake in my life. I'm going to show
you different.* Yeah, and the pressure on us in the 90s is
tremendous because a lot of people just look at us and be
like, "Well, they're not going to make it because they're doing so and so with their lives." And, you know, I'll show
them differently. And they'd be looking at you like, "I
can't believe it." Well, believe it, because I'm going to do
something with my life. It's just a judgment. We're teenagers. Everybody's expecting you to be sleeping around instead of, you know, coming to school, doing your work,
you know, but once you show people that whatever you
say, whatever you do, they can't hurt you [it's OK]. I know
there's plenty of times people doubt, you know, people call

me all kinds of names, and I just looked at them, OK. Once
you show somebody that you really don't care what they
say about you, they want to become your friend then. You
know, "She's got a good head on her shoulders."

Ayisha, through her everyday actions, challenges social representations of teenagers, particularly Black inner-city teenagers who she
thinks are expected to amount to very little. She comes to group,
shares with others, and relishes in the fervent hope that she is going
to make it, in spite of the fact that she had a baby at a young age.
Tia, also in the group, calls her every morning to make sure that she
is coming to school that day and staying "with the program."

Working through sensitive issues cross-race encourages more
open attitudes toward race issues in general, serving to contest and
rewrite social scripts of race difference (Fine, Weis, & Powell, 1997).
Although very little specifically "race work" is done in the group,
such work is very much in the minds of participants. Mindy, a White
young woman from a predominantly Polish area in Buffalo, has this
to say:

Mindy: And my best friend is Black. And a lot of guys from
my neighborhoods try to get with her . . . and they're all
White. It's different . . . a guy will be prejudiced, but he'll
be more prejudiced against a guy that's a different race,
not the girl. You know, it's supposed to be, especially in
my neighborhood, "These [White girls] are *our* girls," you
know. And if you [girls] go outside the neighborhood, they
are mad. The thing about the guys not wanting the girls to
be with people from a different race is because if we're
with guys from a different race, then it kind of leaves them
[White guys] out. I don't know if that makes sense, but
that's the way I look at it. Like a lot of the guys in my
neighborhood expect the girls to be with them, like from
my neighborhood. And they [the guys] can have girls on
the side.
Lois: And these girls—Puerto Rican girls, Black girls, they're
the ones on the side?
Mindy: Uh-huh. And when we're messing with other guys,
whatever, they get so, I don't know, they don't get violent,

but they start saying things like . . . my one friend Jean . . . all she does is date Black people. They'll call her "nigger lover."

Mindy connects racism among neighborhood boys directly with expressed notions of male superiority, with male desires to stake out and control women as property, while at the same time having sex on the side with girls of their choice, often girls of color. She comments further:

> *Mindy*: Like there's this thing now where girls are expected to share boyfriends, especially in my neighborhood. Like you have this boyfriend, but he'll be going out with another girl. But it really doesn't matter, you know, because she's from a different neighborhood, and he'll go to see her on the weekends.
> *Lois*: What about the opposite? Like what about you, if you have more than one boyfriend?
> *Mindy*: That's not how it works. It's kind of going back to the old days, where they're superior.

For Mindy, young men are attempting to stake out the right to have as many women as they want, while at the same time controlling the sexuality of neighborhood girls, authoring them as "sluts" if they see boys outside the neighborhood, particularly boys of color. She understands this as a way of reestablishing male superiority in relationships wherein men/boys control all the actions/desires/sexual behavior of girls/women.

There is some direct, what I call race work, being done in the group, although not much. Most race work takes place around the fact that gendered issues are explored cross-racially and cross-ethnically, serving to rewrite entrenched race scripts. However, the following discussion is an example of race work done directly.

> *Tia*: He's [father] so hard headed, and I think that's where I get my attitude from. He's hard headed. He only wants to think the way he wants to think. And it took him until just now to realize that he can't raise kids [she has ten half brothers and sister, only one full sister who lives with her

and her mom]; he has no patience. His one-year-old daughter, I have more authority than he does. He yells and
screams and loses his mind. But his wife, I had a problem
with. I didn't like her. Because, I don't know why, I think I
didn't like her because she wasn't Black.

Lois: Is she White?

Tiffany: This White girl, like me, isn't it?

Tia: Yes. That's it. I didn't like her. I really did not like her because I thought he could have did a lot better. But the
thing is I had judged her and I apologized to her.

Tiffany: So, do you like her now?

Tia: Yeah, I like her more than my father. And the thing is I
feel kind of bad for her because he's so hardheaded.

Lois: Did you actually apologize to her? Did you say "I didn't
like you?"

Tia: Yes, we have family discussions. We're always talking. I
make him talk. But he judges people, and I've learned to
stop judging people. He still judges people. And he doesn't
like being around White people, but he's married to one.
That's what I don't understand.

Tiffany: That's a hypocrite.

Situated in the middle of a girls' group in a public school, young
women traverse a variety of subjects regarding race, gender, sexuality,
and men. Moving through these issues, under the watchful and caring
eye of Doris Carbonell-Medina, young women begin to form a new
collective—a collective based on a stronger woman/girl, one who is
different in many ways from those left behind emotionally in the
neighborhood. It is a collective that surges cross-race, although not
necessarily in terms of intimate friendships. But these young women,
nevertheless, share the most intimate pieces of themselves in the group
setting, creating a form of friendship that may or may not transcend
the bounds of the school, or even the group. And they think it is
important—they think Womanfocus gives them the space they need
to think things out. And they say:

Tiffany: I think Womanfocus is a good idea. It's good for girls
to talk things out without guys. It's not a man bashing
thing, and it's good.

*   *   *

Mindy: It probably would not change anything (about *whether* to have sex) but it helps us think more. I mean we *should* think more *before* we do things.

*   *   *

Donna: Womanfocus is good. You just sit there with your peers and talk about stuff that's going on. Everybody's going through the same stuff you're going through, so you're not the only one.

*   *   *

Karen: Well it's just fun. Like me and Mindy come down here every day. "Oh yeah, we gotta go." It's fun. It's not only . . . it doesn't like . . . it's just stuff I like, or have thought about. We just talk about it.
Lois: What makes it fun?
Karen: I don't know. It's just fun talking. I like to talk.
Lois: And it doesn't make you nervous to talk about these really intimate things with other people?
Karen: No because I mean I know the kids and, like you and Doris, and you're now, it's not like you're going to go tell everybody.

*   *   *

Kate: I like Womanfocus.
Lois: Yeah?
Kate: Yeah, I think it opened up like a lot, because I got to talk to other people and see how their point of views were so, because I was like the type of person that like, I never really told anybody anything. But it has like, I think it helped me a lot to open up to other people and see how they feel about it and what their point of views are and things.

CONCLUDING

I have focused here on a group within a public school, one that offers opportunities to author alternative gendered and race meanings from those "naturally" distributed in such settings. Doris, being supported by Shirley, the guidance counselor, and the young women discussed here, are working against the grain—challenging representations and inventing new ones, playing with and against taken-for-granted notions of gender, and at times, race, so as to live productive lives free from male abuse. It is the desire to live such lives that brings these young women to this space, a deeply held hope that life can be better than that which they see in much of their surroundings. They are in school, hope to stay there, and want to be different from those youth whom they see as lost. And it is this desire that keeps them coming to group and keeps them talking.

The particular role played by a sexuality education program is important here. In no other area of the school are such intimate subjects discussed. While such discussion might conceivably take place in other small groups of adolescent girls outside of school (there are many such clubs in any community), it is the sexuality education curriculum which offers a concrete space within which many of these issues may be addressed naturally. Relations between the sexes and the rendering problematic of taken-for-granted assumptions about men and women are a natural outgrowth of discussion about sexuality, whether sexuality as related to the use of contraception or a more targeted discussion of abstinence. It is around these issues that conversations can flow freely about "what he wants and expects" and where it is legitimate for young women to draw the line. Issues of alcohol and drug abuse are also easily broached within the whole arena of adolescent sex, as this tangled world for adolescents often involves the expected use of drugs and alcohol. It is no secret that violence often accompanies drug and alcohol use and abuse and that this violence is linked to sex. So the sexuality curriculum offers a unique space for the sort of gender and race work examined here. In no other space does the official curriculum lend itself to these subjects and subsequent potential empowerment for young women. In that sense, then, while the current state of such curriculum in practice may be dismal (Fine, 1988; Trudell, 1993; Whatley, 1991), paradoxically enough, it is this very site that offers possibly some of the greatest potential for important political work. The sexuality curriculum is also a site in which it is legitimate and even encouraged that same-gender groupings prevail. It is these same-gender groupings, once again, that have the greatest potential for interesting curricular work at the same time as they are often the site for the most disappointing activities (Bertram, Marusza, Fine, & Weis, 2000). While the group examined here was not part of the mandated sexuality curriculum in the school, the implications for formal classroom activities are considerable.

The question can be raised, though: To what end does this type of group exist? Do the good parts of the group, the new expressions of collectivity, persist beyond school, or even beyond the group itself? To what extent can such a group *ever* challenge the existing distribution of power and resources, distributions which ultimately determine the lives that these young women will live? In other words, can such a group ever challenge fundamental structural inequalities? Or, does a group like this only put a Band-Aid on a sore, one that cannot be healed by an intervention? To this I can only offer partial answers, of course. There are those who will argue strongly that such groups can never challenge the existing distribution of power and resources in society and therefore can never really do anything for the lives of these girls. In fact, some say, such groups perpetrate only a lie in that they do not really confront the kinds of inequalities facing youth like this, whether along race, social class, or gendered lines. While I may have some sympathy for this argument, ultimately I come down differently on this set of points. These young women are struggling hard to escape what they see as a life filled with exploitation and abuse. They want choices—choices to go to school, to live productively, to live free from male violence and exploitation. And this, to some extent at least, they do control. By beginning the discussion around abuse, by beginning the discussion around victimization, welfare, men, alcoholism, and violence, they gain information, information that many women of our generation did not have. They gain a language—a language of what is abuse, of what is "normal" and what is not in relationships where sex is involved. They hear from trusted adults and their peers what the pitfalls in relationships can be, and what to do when confronted with such pitfalls. What to do with male violence, whether from a boyfriend or a father. What to do when one sees someone else drink too much, or what to do when he has "only hit me once." They hear from Doris, publicly and quickly, that "Believe me, ladies, if he hits you once, he will hit you again." Speaking out and hearing from others also readies young women to continue to do so in the future. If they speak out once, they will be able to speak out again. If they listen to others about sensitive subjects once, they will be able to do so in the future. They will be able to share and build women's communities, communities which support their right to live with respect, free from exploitation and abuse. I and many others like me know that once we speak about horrors and tragedies in our lives, the monkey is off our back—it is easier to speak again. We know that we will not be rejected, be seen as "bad," because of what happened to us. And so these young women will learn, too. By speaking out now, it will be easier to speak out in the future. They have learned that no one will reject them because of what has happened. This represents a form of strength that should never be underestimated. And we, as women, need to continue to speak out, individually and in groups about our shared experiences. But this set of understandings takes many years to come to fruition. These young women have made a beginning in a group designed primarily to encourage abstinence. But a new collective is forming—indeed, one that is based on cross-race interactions and one aimed at understanding and challenging gendered situations and meanings. And so this group is invaluable—it is the beginning of learning to speak out and trust, as we explore ourselves and our position as women.

Revisiting the Struggle for Integration

MICHELLE FINE AND BERNADETTE ANAND

The project we describe in this chapter emerged from thinking about Fridays. While the Monday through Thursday schedule at Renaissance Middle School in Montclair, New Jersey covers the traditional distribution of curriculum, Fridays are dedicated to 9-week cycles of 2-hour sessions. Each session involves in-depth work focusing on five themes: Aviation, Genetics, Building Bridges, Community Service, and this, the Oral History Project. Because the school is thematically organized around core notions of justice, history, social movements, and "renaissances" (that is, Italian, Harlem, and Montclair), we structured this project around the deeply contested history of desegregation of the Montclair public schools.

Renaissance school, like all schools in Montclair, enjoys rich racial and ethnic diversity, the town having been a court-ordered site for desegregation. As of this writing, the school is just 3 years old, with 225 sixth-, seventh-, and eighth-grade students, balanced evenly by gender and by race, with African American and White the primary "racial" codes relied upon by the district. The student body is also diverse in terms of social class, with just under 20% of students eligible for free or reduced lunch.

In a state recognized as the fourth most racially segregated in the nation, in a town well known for its racially integrated schools,

Chapter 7 previously appeared in *Radical Teacher*, (57), pp. 16–20. Used by permission of the Center for Critical Education.

Renaissance is committed to serious intellectual work as well as racial and economic equity. Students' curricula are project-based and inter-disciplinary, and the school is explicitly detracked, with 8 a.m. to 4 p.m. school days. Resources and personnel are directed primarily at instruction: teachers, adults from the community, adjuncts and parent volunteers are relentlessly dedicated to providing strong academic support so that all students can perform meaningful inquiry-based work.

The Civil Rights Oral History project was not, politically or peda-gogically, a departure from the ethical or intellectual stance of the school. As progressive educators, eager for students to engage with historic and contemporary struggles for racial and economic justice, we believed the Civil Rights Oral History Project would prove to be an effective learning experience. Dr. Bernadette Anand was invited to serve as principal of Renaissance based on her reputation as a progressive teacher and principal, a radical critic of tracking, and a supporter of student-based inquiry and multiculturalism; Michelle Fine, a university faculty member, was a parent/volunteer. Together, we constructed the course in that uneasy balance between educator-structured and student-directed learning. As the students moved for-ward, they learned about local history and about themselves as excava-tors of a history rarely told. In this chapter we chronicle the course while identifying key critical turning points and unresolved issues.

We began with a quick immersion into the history of the struggle. We arranged to have *The Montclair Times* scanned for articles relevant to desegregation during the years 1947 to 1972. On the first day of each cycle, students individually reviewed the local newspaper articles tracing Montclair's history of segregation and integration, lawsuits, "riots," the school board plans for incremental integration, the denials of racism, the development of magnet schools and tracking, as well as the stubbornly persistent racial and economic gaps in academic achievement. As they reviewed the newspapers, they began to ask questions along these lines:

- "Why is the Black Student Association protest called a riot—but when the White parents get together to fight integration it's just a parents' meeting?"
- "This town is not only segregated by race, but also by wealth. Which was the problem?"

- "Why do we still sit separately in the lunchroom?"
- "Did the kids have a problem with integration or was it just the parents?"

After some initial instruction and discussion, students were quick to point out the biases of the articles, the journalistic "slants" that accompanied the reporting of the "facts." Some students, particularly a few African-American boys, noticed a disparaging tone toward African-American "student protests" which was absent in the paper's descriptions of White parents' "meetings." Others noted the frequent placement of articles about the Black Student Association near articles about liquor store robberies or drug busts. A few commented that "winners usually write the history." Others concluded, "That's why we have to do this project." Even in the early stages of the project, conflicts arose as we discussed past controversies. We strove to set a distinct tone: one of respect for all points of view.

In preparation for the interviews, we watched portions of *Eyes on the Prize*, read *Freedom's Children*, and discussed these histories of racism in two Southern states, Arkansas and Alabama. Students were shocked by the brutality of Little Rock and awed by the strength shown by protesters and those who refused to take "no" for an answer. The class then listened to Montclair's own: Arthur Kinoy, civil rights activist and lawyer, who riveted us with national and local stories about oppression, resistance, and McCarthyism. Kinoy's enthusiasm came across in the laughter that punctuated his tough talk of blacklisting, institutional and state-sponsored exclusions. He reminded us that struggle and protest are lifelong work. Students soon learned that it wasn't only the South that was ambivalent about or hostile to integration. As they read and reread the newspapers, they came to see the use of phrases like "neighborhood schools," "worries about small children on buses" or "community control" as polite ways for community members to insist on segregated schools. Students quickly saw how fundamentally race was inscribed in the history of our town.

With the archive of these articles in hand, the class worked together to produce a time line of the major segregation and desegregation events. From the creation of this time line onward, the structure of the course evolved according to the students' interests. They identified key players from the newspaper articles and then recruited widely for a broad sample of potential interviewees. Early in the fall, a small group of students wrote a letter that appeared in the local newspaper inviting bus drivers, teachers, students, crossing guards, shopkeepers, parents, children, and teachers who observed or participated in the late 1960s integration struggles to contact the school for an interview. Over 20 interviews were completed during the course of the school year.

With our guidance and that of their peers, students prepared themselves for the interview process. They generated the questions to be asked and role-played the passive or reticent interviewee as well as the one who wouldn't shut up. We explained that oral history interviews should be designed to elicit personal stories, filled with contradiction, varied perspectives, and layered experiences. We sought variety, not consensus. We were all surprised at the level of sophistication and honesty students brought to the project, as evidenced by the tough questions they composed: "Did the teachers take out their anger on you because you were 'colored'? Did other kids, I mean White kids, invite you to their house for dinner?" "Were you upset that your parents brought a lawsuit?"

In preparing for the interviews, there was a long and sometimes difficult conversation about language, focusing specifically on whether students should use "colored," "Negro" (the vernacular of the times), "Black," or "African-American" in the interviews. One student asked if it would be appropriate to use "Nigger," a term he relies upon to signal endearment and friendship, seemingly naive about its history. The class argued with varied points of view. We decided, ultimately, out of respect for our interviewees, we wouldn't use Nigger, but "colored" or "Negro" would be acceptable if the interviewees used that language first.

Later in the year, this conversation was resurrected, this time specifically about the use of "Nigger" or "Nigga," by and among African-American boys and their music. Allie Baskerville, the grandson of one of the women who initially brought the lawsuit for desegregation in 1967, had just conducted a phone interview with his grandmother about the litigation. After hanging up, he turned to Bernadette and some friends and asked, almost innocently, "You know, given what my grandmother and her friends did, how come we use Nigger so easily, when it was used to put us down?"

Students were also surprised and provoked by some of the interview material. They expected stories about discrimination from Whites and solidarity among Blacks. But when the students asked a number of the then-Negro-children, "Were the White children nice to you?" they were surprised to hear from two respondents, "Some of the White children were better friends to me than some of the other Negro children." A difficult conversation ensued as White, African-American, and biracial children wondered, "Why would other Black children be mad that you were doing well in school, and resent that you were a cheerleader?" Two African-American students admitted that it was "hard to talk about that in front of some of the White kids." Stories of intraracial struggles moved to the surface, sharing the floor with stories of interracial conflicts. On a visit to Renaissance, an African-American teacher from Connecticut admitted to her discomfort when she listened to a light-skinned respondent recall, "I remember being invited, often, to many white homes for sleepovers . . . " This teacher recalled White girls' shunning her in the 1950s. "Try havin' nappy hair and real dark skin and see if you got invited," she remarked to the class. Her comments sparked conversations about skin color, "good hair," and who gets invited to which sleepovers.

And then there were just the chilling, recognizable historic revelations about our town that shivered through the class. During an interview with Lydia Davis-Barrett, once a child in the Montclair public schools and currently the director of the Essex County Urban League, students learned:

> So we decided to go to the White people's pool to take lessons—boy were they surprised to see us, but they just said, "You sure you're in the right place?" to which we said that we were sure. But what hurt me so, as I approached the pool, is that I realized in the colored people's pool we had to dip our feet in a bucket of disinfectant . . . no such rule in the White people's pool.

Davis-Barrett continued:

> I graduated first in my class, or so I thought from Glenfield and then I got to the high school and I was getting D's. I didn't understand it, and my father was mad. He tried to find out what was going on. Was I messing up? Were the teachers racist? And then he discovered that I was first in my class, at least first among the colored children, but we were given a "colored" curriculum at Glenfield. We weren't getting the same

rigor, the same courses as the White children, so of course once
I got to the high school I was way behind. . . . My dad wanted
to bring a lawsuit but he was a civil servant and they told him
if he did, he would lose his job.

Students sat stunned and open-mouthed. Some were disbelieving,
while others were familiarly pained.

An important set of pedagogical turns emerged as we realized
the unconscious assumptions that infused our work. When students
sympathetically asked some of the children of activists, "Was it difficult being the child of an activist?" they learned that their worries
were misguided. We had all assumed the litigation was difficult and
embarrassing, and we prepared questions that were appropriately
sensitive. However, most of the men and women who were intimately
involved said the lawsuit was "thrilling . . . I knew they [my parents]
loved me because they were willing to take up the fight." We had to
go back to our interview protocol and reassess the biases in all of our
questions and search for other buried assumptions.

In interviews with African-American and White men and women
educators, parents, activists, then children in the schools, we heard
detailed stories of White resistance to integration, some surprising
White support for integration and opposition to community schools,
complex reactions to desegregation within the African-American community, and the delights and the vulnerabilities of having a "mixed"
group of friends. We heard about "colored" support for integration
and about economic and political tensions within the Black community. We learned about housing segregation seemingly so hard to undo
that schools became the site of the struggle for desegregation. We
questioned why the schools built in the "Negro" section of town were
so well equipped with gyms, equipment, theaters, music and dance
studios, especially compared to the schools in the "White" section of
town. We then realized that the school board assumed, and they were
probably right, that some White people had to be bribed into putting
their children on a bus to go to the "other" side of town. Throughout
the interviews, it seemed painfully clear that most White children were
going to get a good education, integration or not. On the other hand,
African-American students who had lost opportunities during segregation experienced a new kind of racism, confronted a more veiled form
of segregation through tracking, even after the victory in 1967.

A memorable moment came when students interviewed Dr. Mindy Fullilove. A psychiatrist at Columbia-Presbyterian, Dr. Fullilove is the daughter of a civil rights activist from a neighboring town, the daughter who used to "skip to school as a young child, loving every day." She knew as a child that her father was involved with a civil rights struggle in his town of Orange, New Jersey. She didn't know, however, that if he won, she would have to go to school with White children. He won. Dr. Fullilove told the seventh graders, "integration almost killed me." At that moment we realized that an unspoken, unchallenged bias floated in the room and saturated our interviews: *that segregation was bad and integration was good.* Unacknowledged was the pain, the loss, the questionable consequences of integration, especially for African-American children, families, and teachers. We spent much time reviewing how every so-called solution to social injustice brings with it other burdens, other struggles. We realized that African Americans in the Americas can never rest assured that racism has been put in its place. Just as painful, we saw that racism and White supremacy do not disappear after integration; they merely take new forms.

But insights never come easily and they don't come to everyone at the same time in the same way. There were significant points of discensus among us for which we, as educators, had to create room and respect, as well as analysis. For example, Kaelin (White girl) and Trevor (biracial boy) argued powerfully and with conviction about how to ask about "teachers" after integration. Kaelin preferred what she thought was a "neutral" question like, "What were the teachers like after integration?" Trevor preferred what he thought was a more directed, even sharply pointed question: "Did the teachers take out their anger on you because you were colored?" We spent a full session discussing the politics of their questions and why Kaelin would want "nice" data and Trevor might want evidence of struggle. Kaelin knew she was looking for some evidence of White adults who fought against racism and Trevor knew he was looking for evidence about the pain of integration. Both knew that if they didn't ask (for the good news or the bad), these memories might never be reported. We asked the question both ways and got wildly different responses. We recognized that how you ask a question affects what you get in response.

A few weeks later, students in the class were asked to describe the project to a newspaper reporter from *The Newark Star Ledger* who had learned about the project through the students' open letter to the

The Montclair Times. Here, too, the students' racialized postures were evident. One White student said, "It was interesting, really, to hear that people in town didn't know the schools were segregated. They didn't know anything was wrong." An African-American boy interrupted, "Lots of people *knew* something was wrong but they didn't know *what to do* about it." Even at the end of the year, in thinking about the dramatic differences between interviews with White and African-American women activists, we continued to note the differences in our own reactions to what we were hearing. Michelle asked, "What differences did you notice in these interviews?" A White girl responded, "It was harder for White people to be involved in the protests because they lost friends." At the same moment an African-American boy responded, "White people who were involved took all the credit." We analyzed again what the women said in the interviews and then what we heard. In our analysis we noticed a story within a story: a tale of race, class, and gender in our past and a tale of race, class, and gender in our midst. That is, we spent much time trying to figure out how each of the interviewees *and* each of us constructs narratives of our lives and our politics; how profoundly our race, class, and gender positions influence what we hear, and how we frame and interpret issues of social (in)justice.

Throughout the year, students came to see that what is taken for granted today in their lives has a long history of national and local struggles. Some went home and asked their parents about going to Montclair High School in the 1960s. Others gathered stories about segregated schools in the South. They started to question their own lunchroom and their future. What's going to happen when we hit high school, will we "split" again by race? Why were some Whites so scared to go to school with Blacks? Why were some Black students so hard on other Black children who were academic achievers? Why were there so few Black educators then and still today? As educators, Bernadette and Michelle noticed that there were, and are, conversations still too terrifying to wander into, assumptions too horrifying to challenge, such as: What counts as smart—and is it genetic? What about all those teachers who encouraged some students to believe they were smart and others to believe they were not adequate? What are the peer costs of being academically engaged for African-American children? How do we make sense of the racial segregation of Special Education? What does it mean to be biracial, part White and part

Black, or part Asian and part Black, or part White and Latino, in this conversation? Why is "basic skills" so segregated? How does social class interact with race and ethnicity in this town, and in this country? Why do people judge students whose friends are from different races? What happens when we have to decide *whose* music to play at the dance? *And ultimately, we all had to reflect on a question we didn't entertain at the beginning of the year: Is integration really better?*

For some students, this project simply reiterated a history of struggle that has been their family's history of struggle. It was in their blood, their legacy, discussed over the dinner table. For others it was new and painful, awkward or even embarrassing. White students and educators had to figure out what kind of legacy we brought to the table; African-American students and educators had to confront tough evidence of separation, hatred, and denial of opportunity burned into their collective memory; biracial students, Asian and Latino students had to carve a place for themselves in this history. All students had to assess their own relation to this struggle. No one, of course, wanted to see themselves or their kin as "bad guys," eager to perpetuate unequal racial and economic opportunities. But then the conversation turned to what you do if you *witness* unequal or unfair treatment of a student by a teacher, by another classmate, or a stranger. Do you simply watch and turn? Do you intervene? Do you tell a teacher? Do you encourage it?

"By witnessing passively," someone remarked, "if we do nothing, then it keeps going on. I mean, we allow it to get worse." And so these young people in the 1990s, the children of the generation who fought so many of these battles, by year's end began to confront the ongoing politics of race, class, and gender. To this list they added the politics of "being fat," "having bad clothes," "stuttering," "not being very masculine," "they say I'm gay," "not having a mother," "having big breasts," and, as always, "where we sit in the lunchroom."

*   *   *

Months into the course, three African-American boys from sixth and seventh grade were stopped by the police while walking home. Their backpacks were searched. Apparently a passerby had called the police and said that a group of boys—one of whom had a gun—were throwing snowballs. Unsuspecting, these boys had stopped to purchase some gum. When the police insisted that they stand still to be frisked, a young White girl from Renaissance, on her way to dance class, saw the confrontation. She had her mother call Bernadette Anand immediately because she knew something was wrong. She would not "witness passively."

As it turned out, the boys were entirely innocent and the police were asked to come to the school to speak with the school community, including the three boys and their parents. Students, parents, and faculty across the school engaged in an analysis of the history, politics, and practices of police harassment of children of color. This occurred only 2 days after the Amadu Diallo murder in New York City, when an innocent African man was gunned down by police, killed with over 40 bullets, in a case of mistaken identification.

Today, students and faculty are organizing a strategy for a delegation of Renaissance students and faculty to visit stores that are "discriminately suspect" of youths. Some students are conducting community-based research in which White and African-American students enter a particular store and the "researcher" documents who is followed, who is asked to leave, who is asked for help. They are keeping notes, honing their research and activist skills.

We are now well beyond the years of formal segregation, post–civil rights, thriving in a town well known for its embrace of integration. Indeed, Montclair has been recognized by *New Jersey Magazine* as one of the "nation's best towns for multi-racial families." Yet boys of color are still particularly vulnerable to police surveillance and harassment. But what separates this school from most is that here the administration and faculty decided this police search constituted an assault against the schoolwide community, an issue in need of historic and social analysis, a dynamic to be studied and halted. A White girl witnessed and reported. The three boys and their families were embraced by a school collectively experiencing the pain. An African-American police officer came to address the school, relating his own experiences of brutality suffered as a youth, at the hands of police officers, noting that that was the moment when he decided to become an officer himself. At Renaissance Middle School, as part of their formal and informal educations, young people across racial and ethnic groups, across economic categories and neighborhoods, learn intimately and critically about the scars of exclusion and oppression, in the past as well as today. They learn, too, that research, resistance,

and community organizing are an ongoing part of life for those concerned with social justice.

When we think now about the class, we notice an interesting
pattern. In the fall, there was, discernibly, uneven participation. African-American boys were much more likely to be involved in the
classroom conversations than any other demographic "group" in the
room: eager to talk, interview, generate questions, and probe more
fully. While everyone participated some—given the nature of the
project, everyone had to generate questions and conduct interviews—
initially it seemed toughest for some of the White boys to engage.
Understanding discrimination firsthand or even secondhand from
family and friends were critical "assets" in this project. Students who
had an "eye" for injustice, had been educated around the dinner table
or perhaps had been scrutinized by mall security and surveillance,
were most ready to do the research and analysis. Over time, however,
with practice at interviewing and being interviewed, independent
researching and analyzing the transcripts, engagement was much
more even. Eventually, whether they were creating questions, conducting interviews, transcribing, writing the preface to the book, titling
the book (*Montclair Wrong for Too Long: The Struggles for Integration*)
or figuring out the table of contents, most students became actively
engaged, demonstrating their curiosity and wisdom.

*   *   *

On the last morning of the interviewing phase of the project, two
women were scheduled for interviews. We spoke first with a White
woman, now retired, who fought hard for integration as a mother of
an adolescent in the early 1970s. We then talked to an older African-
American woman, a university professor, who also fought hard, at
the same time, as a parent and community member. Each was asked,
in seventh-grade dialect, "So, was life better before integration or
after?" The first woman, without hesitation, exclaimed, "Much better
after!" The students go to school together, they have play dates, they
are no longer separated." And the second woman explained, after a
long pause, "Neither was better. The struggle continues." Students
learned that both answers were, in their time and for each of these
women, respectively, "true."

A Memo to Educators

Lois Weis and Michelle Fine

We finish this book post-September 11, 2001. From the ashes, in the urban Northeast, rises a sense of urgency about persistent social injustices, both global and national, rooted in economic, racial, ethnic, gender, and sexuality relations; the growing gap between the "haves" and the "have nots." Schools, like other public institutions organized by the state, represent these relations of perverse imbalance. Travel 20 minutes north from the South Bronx to schools in suburban Westchester County, visit a public school on the Lower East Side of New York and a private school blocks away, and it's hard to call them all "school." The "achievement gap" is international and local; it signifies massive social injustice and local tragedy, woven into the very structures, policies, practices, interactions, and identities that constitute schooling.

And so arises the question, What are the responsibilities of urban educators? In a world in which racial, ethnic, class, gender, and sexuality inequities are painfully apparent, in which public education survives as the last institution designed for all, the call to teachers rings urgent and passionate. It demands courage. As the early essays in this book testify, we recognize that in America teachers need to do nothing in order for "reproduction" of social inequities to persist. As Beverly Tatum argues, racism is like the "moving walkway" in airports. Just stop on and go for the ride. If you simply stand still, existing structures, policies, and practices—masquerading as "neutral"—will assure that bad things will (continue to) happen, for most poor and working-class youth.

This book seeks to acknowledge this very typicality of "reproduction," while at the same time inspire an alternative posture from educators—a recognition of and invitation toward the powerful work "against the grain" (Cochran-Smith & Lytle, 1992) undertaken by so many educators and youth workers in supportive, but far more often unsupportive, environments. At the moment, as the numbers of juveniles in criminal justice facilities swell, as high-stakes testing proliferates and dropout rates spike for the first time in a decade, we recognize that the costs of inequitable and damaging public education are painfully high for poor youth, and particularly youth of color in urban America. We write with recognition that educational practice for justice is hard, but it is essential.

We end with a sense of hope. Today's youth—those living in poverty and wealth; in urban, suburban, and rural communities; those who are White, African American, Latino, Asian, native born, and immigrant—if they have been raised in America, have matured in a time of a shrinking public sphere and a narrowed sense of the common good. And yet we have evidence that these same youth flourish when challenged intellectually to engage with rigor and possibility, within those spaces we call public schools. Such students deserve so much more than we have delivered to them. This book is dedicated to youth who persist in spite of the odds, to those who have (hopefully temporarily) given up, and the educators who have stood by all of them.

Notes

Chapter 1

1. This research was made possible by a grant from the W. T. Grant Foundation, New York City, 1984 through 1985.

2. Personal communication with employee in the High Schools' Division, New York City Board of Education, in response to inquiry about why New York City does not maintain race/ethnicity sensitive statistics on dropping out and school achievement.

Chapter 2

1. The research reported in this chapter represents one component of a year-long ethnographic investigation of students and dropouts at a comprehensive public high school in New York City. Funded by the W. T. Grant Foundation, the research was designed to investigate how public urban high schools produce dropout rates in excess of 50%. The methods employed over the year included: in-school observations four days per week during the fall, and one to two days per week during the spring; regular (daily) attendance in a hygiene course for twelfth graders; an archival analysis of more than 1,200 students who compose the 1978-79 cohort of incoming ninth graders; interviews with approximately 55 recent and long-term dropouts; analysis of fictional and autobiographical writings by students; a survey distributed to a sub-sample of the cohort population; and visits to proprietary schools, programs for Graduate Equivalency Diplomas, naval recruitment sites, and a public high school for pregnant and parenting teens. The methods and preliminary results of the ethnography are detailed in Fine, 1986.

2. This information is derived from personal communications with former and present employees of major urban school districts who have chosen to remain anonymous.

3. Personal communication.

Chapter 3

1. The Preliminary Scholastic Aptitude Test (PSAT) and Scholastic Aptitude Test (SAT) are administered by the Educational Testing Service in Princeton. Most 4-year colleges require the SAT for entrance.

2. The governing body of the state educational system administers a series of tests that must be taken in high school if entrance to a 4-year college is desired. Not all students take these tests, of course; the track placement often determines whether the tests are taken.

Chapter 4

1. My thanks to Allen Hunter for making this point.

Chapter 6

1. This move to filter massive funding into abstinence only programming is reflected in state RFPs. New York, for example, where this research was conducted, released an RFP on February 17, 1998, noting that "approximately $4.5 million dollars are available for this initiative, which will support a range of 20–30 funded projects. The range of funding awards is anticipated to be $100,000 to $200,000; the average award is anticipated to be $150,000" (p. 4). Abstinence education, for the purpose of this RFP, has the following components:

(A) has as its exclusive purpose teaching the social, psychological, and health gains to be realized by abstaining from sexual activity;

(B) teaches abstinence from sexual activity outside marriage as the expected standard for all school-age children;

(C) teaches that abstinence from sexual activity is the only certain way to avoid out-of-wedlock pregnancy, sexually transmitted diseases, and other associated health problems;

(D) teaches that a mutually faithful monogamous relation in the context of marriage is the expected standard of human sexual activity;

(E) teaches that sexual activity outside the context of marriage is likely to have harmful psychological and physical effects;

(F) teaches that bearing children out of wedlock is likely to have harmful consequences for the child, the child's parents, and society;

(G) teaches young people how to reject sexual advances and how alcohol and drug use increase vulnerability to sexual advances; and

(H) teaches the importance of attaining self-sufficiency before engaging in sexual activity.

2. An important exception to the statement is the work by Bonnie Nelson Trudell. Trudell carefully focused on the day-to-day workings of such programs.

3. The program studied here is an abstinence-based program whose funding source is Buffalo Adolescent Pregnancy Prevention Services, as funded by the Office of Child and Family Services (formerly Department of Social Services).

4. My Bottom Line is under the auspices of Womanfocus, a program stem in the larger Preventionfocus, which receives much of its money from the New York State Office of Alcoholism and Substance Abuse Services. Preventionfocus is aimed at promoting healthy lifestyles throughout the life cycle, through prevention of drug, alcohol, and substance abuse and early pregnancy.

5. Doris Carbonell-Medina, Esq., has her J.D. from SUNY Buffalo Faculty of Law and Jurisprudence and is licensed to practice law in New York State. Before working for Preventionfocus, where she runs most of the workshops connected to Womanfocus, she worked with Prisoners Legal Services of New York and was in private legal practice. Her legal expertise consists of civil rights litigation, including work in employment discrimination, police brutality, family law, and entertainment law. She currently practices law on a referral basis only.

References

Advocates for Children. (1985). *Report of the New York hearings on the crisis in public education*. New York.

Anand, B., Fine, M., Perkins, T. & Surrey, S. (2002). *Keeping the struggle alive: Studying desegregation in our town: A guide to doing oral history*. New York: Teachers College Press.

Anaya, R. A. (1991). *The legend of La Llorona: A short novel*. Berkeley, CA: TQS Publications.

Anyon, J. (1980, Spring). School curriculum: Political and economic structure and social change. *Social Practice*, 96–108.

Anyon, J.(1981). Social class and school knowledge. *Curriculum Inquiry, 11*(1), 3–42.

Anyon, J. (1982). Social class and the hidden curriculum of work. *Journal of Education, 162* (1), 67–92.

Anyon, J. (1983). Intersections of gender and class: Accommodation and resistance by working class and affluent females to contradictory sex role ideologies. In S. Walker and L. Barton (Eds.), *Gender, class and education*. (pp. 19–38). London: Falmer Press.

Anyon, J. (1997). *Ghetto schooling: A political economy of urban educational reform*. New York: Teachers College Press.

Apfelbaum, E. (1979). Relations of domination and movement for liberation: An analysis of power between groups. In W. G. Austin & S. Worchel (Eds.), *The social psychology of intergroup relations* (pp. 188–204). Belmont, CA: Wadsworth.

Apple, M. W. (1979). *Ideology and curriculum*. London: Routledge & Kegan Paul.

Apple, M. W. (1982a). *Cultural and economic reproduction in education*. Boston: Routledge and Kegan Paul.

Apple, M. W. (1982b). *Education and power*. Boston: Routledge & Kegan Paul.

Apple, M. W. (1983). Curriculum form and the logic of technical control. In M. W. Apple & L. Weis (Eds.), *Ideology and practice in schooling*(pp. 143–166). Philadelphia: Temple University Press.

Apple, M. W. (2000). *Official knowledge: Democratic education in a conservative age*. New York: Routledge.

Aronowitz, S., & Giroux, H. A. (1985). *Education under siege*. South Hadley, MA: Bergin & Garvey.

Aronowitz, S., and Giroux, H.A. (1993). Education still under siege. (2nd ed.) Westport, Conn.: Bergin & Garvey.

Aspira of New York. (1983). *Racial and ethnic high school dropout rates in New York City: A summary report*. New York. State University of New York Press.

Ayers, B. (1960). *Education: An American problem*. Boston, MA: New England Free Press.

Ayers, R., Ayers, W., Dohrn, B. & Jackson, T. (2001). *Zero tolerance*. New York: The New Press.

Ayers, W., Klonsky, M., & Lyon, G. (2000). (Eds.). *A simple justice: The challenge of small schools* (pp. 13–17). New York: Teachers College Press.

Banks, J. (1992, July/September).Authentic science and school science. *International Journal of Science Education, 14*, 265–272.

Banks, J. (1997). *Educating citizens in a multicultural society*. New York: Teachers College Press.

Banks, J. & McGee Banks, C. (1995). *Handbook of research on multicultural education*. New York: Macmillan.

Barry, R. (2000). Sheltered "children:" The self-creation of a safe space by gay, lesbian, and bisexual students. In L. Weis & M. Fine (Eds.), *Construction sites* (pp. 84–99). New York: Teachers College Press.

Bastian, A., Fruchter, N., Gittell, M., Greer, C., & Haskins, K. (1985, Spring). Choosing equality: The case for democratic schooling. *Social Policy, 35*–51.

Bauer, G. (1986). *The family: Preserving America's future*. Washington DC: U.S. Department of Education.

Benedetto, R. (1987, January 23). AIDS studies become part of curricula. *USA Today*, p. D1.

Benjamin, J. (1983). Master and slave: The fantasy of erotic domination. In A. Snitow, C. Stansell, & S. Thompson (Eds.), *Powers of desire*. (pp. 280–299). New York: Monthly Review Press.

Bennett, W. (1987, July 3). Why Johnny can't abstain. *National Review, 56*, 36–38.

Bernstein, B. (1977). *Class, codes and control*. (Vol. 3). London: Routledge & Kegan Paul.

Bertram, C., Marusza, J., Fine, M., & Weis, L. (2000). Where the girls (women) are. *Journal of Community Psychology, 28*(5),731–755.

Bigelow, M. (1921). *Sex-Education*. New York: Macmillan.

Billig, M. (1995). *Banal nationalism*. London: Sage.

Boffey, P. (1987, February 27). Reagan to back AIDS plan urging youths to avoid sex. *New York Times*. p. A14.

Bourdieu, P. (1991). *Symbolic power*. Cambridge, MA: Harvard University Press.

Bourdieu, P. & Passeron, J. C. (1977). *Reproduction in education, society and culture*. London: Sage.

Bowen, W. G., & Bok, D. C. (1998). *The shape of the river: Long-term consequences of considering race in college and university admissions*. Princeton, NJ: Princeton University Press.

Bowles, S., & Gintis, H. (1976). *Schooling in capitalist America: Educational reform and the contradictions of economic life*. New York: Basic Books.

Brown, P. (1983). The Swedish approach to sex education and adolescent pregnancy: Some impressions. *Family Planning Perspectives, 15*(2), 92–95.

Burdell, P. (1998, February). Young mothers as students: Moving toward a new century. *Education and Urban Society, 30*(2): 207–223.

Burke, C. (1980). Introduction to Luce Irigaray's "When our lips speak together." *Signs, 6*, 66–68.

Burt, M., Kimmich, M., Goldmuntz, J., & Sonnenstein, F. (1984). *Helping pregnant adolescents: Outcomes and costs of service delivery. Final Report on the Evaluation of Adolescent Pregnancy Programs*. Washington, DC: Urban Institute.

Cardinale, A. (2002, May 15). Math A Exam woes add up to frustration. *Buffalo News*, p. B3.

Carnegie Forum of Education and the Economy. (1986). *A nation prepared: Teachers for the 21st century*. New York: Carnegie Foundation.

Carnoy, M., & Levin, H. (1985). *Schooling and work in the democratic state*. Stanford, CA: Stanford University Press.

Cartoof, V., & Klerman, L. (1986). Parental consent for abortion: Impact of the Massachusetts law. *American Journal of Public Health, 76*, 397–400.

Chicago school clinic is sued over birth control materials. (1986, October 16). *New York Times*, p. A24.

Children's Defense Fund. (1986). *Preventing adolescent pregnancy: What schools can do*. Washington, DC: Author.

Children's Defense Fund. (1987). *Adolescent pregnancy: An anatomy of a social problem in search of comprehensive solutions*. Washington, DC: Author.

Cixous, H. (1981). Castration or decapitation? *Signs, 7*, 41–55.

Cochran-Smith, M., & Lytle, S. (1992). Interrogating cultural diversity: Inquiry and action. *Journal of Teacher Education, 43*, 104–115.

Connell, R., Ashenden, D., Kessler, S., & Dowsett, G. (1982). *Making the Difference*. Sydney, Australia: George Allen & Unwin.

Cook, A. (2000). Small schools essay. In E. Clinchy (Ed.), *Creating new schools: How small schools are changing American Education*. New York: Teachers College Press.

Cornbleth, C. (1990). *Curriculum in context*. New York: Falmer Press.

Cummins, J. (1986, February). Empowering minority students: A framework for intervention. *Harvard Education Review, 56*(1),18–36.

Darling-Hammond, L. (2001). The challenge of staffing our schools. *Educational Leadership, 58*(8), 12–17.

Davidson, A. L. (1996). *Making and molding identity in schools.* Albany: State University of New York Press.

Dawson, D. (1986). The effects of sex education on adolescent behavior. *Family Planning Perspectives, 18,* 162–170.

Delpit, L. (1988). The silenced dialogue: Power and pedagogy in educating other people's children. *Harvard Educational Review, 58,* 280–298.

Dowd, M. (1986, April 16). Bid to update sex education confronts resistance in city. *New York Times,* p. A1.

Dryfoos, J. (1985a). A time for new thinking about teenage pregnancy. *American Journal of Public Health, 75,* 13–14.

Dryfoos, J. (1985b). School-based health clinics: A new approach to preventing adolescent pregnancy? *Family Planning Perspectives, 17*(2), 70–75.

DuBois, W. E. B. (1935). Does the Negro need separate schools? *Journal of Negro Education, 4,* 328–335.

Ehrenreich, B., Hess, E., & Jacobs, G. (1986). *Re-making love.* Garden City, NY: Anchor Press.

Elliott, D., Voss, H., & Wendling, A. (1966). Capable dropouts and the social milieu of high school. *Journal of Educational Research, 60,* 180–186.

Ellsworth, E. (1989). Why doesn't this feel empowering?: Working through the repressive myths of critical pedagogy. *Harvard Educational Review, 59,* 297–324.

Emihovich, C. (1998, February). Framing—teen parenting. *Education and Urban Society. 30*(2), 139–156.

Espin, O. (1984). Cultural and historical influences on sexuality in Hispanic/ Latina women: Implications for psychotherapy. In C. Vance (Ed.), *Pleasure and danger* (pp. 149–164). Boston: Routledge & Kegan Paul.

Evans, S., & Boyte, H. (1992). *Free spaces.* Chicago: University of Chicago Press.

Fanon, F. (1967). *Black skin, white masks.* New York: Grove Press.

Felice, J. (1981). Black student dropout behaviors: Disengagement from school rejection and racial discrimination. *Journal of Negro Education, 50,* 415–424.

Fine, M. (1983). Perspectives on inequity: Voices from urban schools. In L. Bickman (Ed.), *Applied Social Psychology Annual IV.* Beverly Hills, CA: Sage.

Fine, M. (1985, Fall). Dropping out of high school: An inside look. *Social Policy,* 43–50.

Fine, M. (1986). Why urban adolescents drop into and out of high school. *Teachers College Record, 87,* 393–409.

Fine, M. (1987). Silencing in public school. *Language Arts, 64,* 157–174.

Fine, M. (1988). Sexuality, schooling and adolescent females: The missing discourse of desire. *Harvard Educational Review, 58*, 29–53.

Fine, M. (1991). *Framing dropouts*. Albany: State University of New York Press.

Fine, M. (1992). *Disruptive voices: The possibilities of feminist research*. Ann Arbor: University of Michigan Press.

Fine, M. (1993). Apparent involvement: Reflections on parents, power, and urban public schools. *Teachers College Record, 94*, 682–710.

Fine, M., Anand, B., Jordan, C., & Sherman, D. (2000). Before the bleach gets us all. In Weis, L., & Fine, M. (Eds.), *Construction sites* (pp. 161–179). New York: Teachers College Press.

Fine, M., & Rosenberg, P. (1983). Dropping out of high school: The ideology of school and work. *Journal of Education, 165*, 257–272.

Fine, M., & Somerville, J. (Eds.). (1998). *Small schools, big imaginations*. Chicago: Cross City Campaign for Urban Education Reform.

Fine, M., & Weis, L. (1998). *The unknown city: The voices of poor and working class young adults*. Boston: Beacon Press.

Fine, M., & Weis, L. (2000). *Construction sites: Excavating race, class and gender*. New York: Teachers College Press.

Fine, M., Weis, L., Centrie, C., & Roberts, R. (2000). Educating beyond the borders of schooling. *Anthropology and Education Quarterly, 31*(2), 131–151.

Fine, M., Weis, L., & Powell, L. (1997). Communities of difference. *Harvard Educational Review, 67*(2), 247–284.

Fisher, W., Byrne, D., & White, L. (1983). Emotional barriers to contraception. In D. Byrne & W. Fisher (Eds.), *Adolescents, sex, and contraception* (pp. 207–239). Hillsdale, NJ: Lawrence Erlbaum.

Foster, M. (1997). *Black teachers on teaching*. New York: New Press.

Foucault, M. (1977). *Discipline and punish: The birth of the prison*. New York: Pantheon.

Foucault, M. (1980). *The history of sexuality* (Vol. 1). New York: Vintage Press.

Foucault, M. (1990). *The history of sexuality: An introduction*. New York: Vintage Books.

Fraser, N. (1990). Rethinking the public sphere: A contribution to the critique of actually existing democracy. *Social Text, 8–9*, 56–80.

Fraser, N. (1993). Rethinking the public sphere. In Robbins, B. (Ed.), *The phantom public sphere*. Minneapolis: University of Minnesota Press.

Freire, P. (1970). *Pedagogy of the oppressed*. New York: Herder & Herder.

Freire, P. (1985). *The politics of education*. South Hadley, MA: Bergin & Garvey.

Freire, P. (1989). *Pedagogy of the Oppressed* (pp. 19–25, 27–56, 75–118). New York: Continuum.

Freudenberg, N. (1987). The politics of sex education. *HealthPAC Bulletin*. New York: HealthPAC.

Friend, R. (1993). In Weis, L., & Fine, M. (Eds.), *Beyond silenced voices: Class, race and gender in U.S. schools* (pp. 237–258). Albany, New York: State University of New York Press.

Gambrell, A., & Haffner, D. (1993). *Unfinished business: A SIECUS assessment of state sexuality education programs.* New York: SIECUS, as cited in Wilcox (1998).

Gaskell, J. (1992). *Gender matters from school to work.* Philadelphia: Open University Press.

Gilgamesh: A new rendering in English verse. (1992). New York: Farrar, Straus & Giroux.

Ginsburg, M. (1988). *Contradictions in teacher education and society: A critical analysis.* New York: Falmer Press.

Giroux, H. (1983a). Theories of reproduction and resistence in the new schooling of education: A critical analysis. *Harvard Educational Review, 53,* 257–293.

Giroux, H. (1983b). *Theory and resistance in education.* South Hadley, MA: Bergin & Garvey.

Giroux, H. (1988). Literacy and the pedagogy of voice and political empowerment. *Educational Theory, 38,* 61–75.

Giroux, H. (1991). *Postmodernism, feminism and cultural politics.* Albany: State University of New York Press.

Giroux, H., & McLaren, P. (1986, August). Teacher education and the politics of engagement. *Harvard Educational Review, 56*(3), 213–238.

Giroux, H. A., & McLaren, P. (Eds.). (1994). *Between borders : Pedagogy and the politics of cultural studies.* New York: Routledge.

Goodlad, J. (1984). *A place called school: Prospects for the future.* New York: McGraw-Hill.

Gramsci, A. (1971). *Selections from prison notebooks.* New York: International.

Grant, C., & Sleeter, C. (1986, Summer). Educational equity: Education that is multicultural and social reconstructionist. *Journal of Educational Equity and Leadership, 6*(2), 106–118.

Greene, M. (1980). Aesthetics and the experience of the arts: Towards transformations. *High School Journal, 63*(8), 316–322.

Greene, M. (1986). In search of a critical pedagogy. *Harvard Educational Review, 56,* 427–441.

Greene, M. (1995). *Releasing the imagination.* San Francisco: Jossey-Bass.

Greene, M. (2000). Lived spaces, shared spaces, public spaces. In L. Weis & M. Fine (Eds.), *Construction sites* (pp. 293–303). New York: Teachers College Press.

Greene, M. (2001). *Variations on a blue guitar: The Lincoln Center Institute lectures on aesthetic education.* New York: Teachers College Press.

Hall, G. S. (1914, December 1). Education and the social hygiene movement. *Social Hygiene, 1,* 29–35.

Haney, W. (1993). Testing and minorities. In L. Weis & M. Fine (Eds.), *Beyond silenced voices: Class, race, and gender in United States schools.* Albany: State University of New York Press.

Haney, W. (2001). *Report on the case of New York performance standards.* Paper presented at Consortium v. Commissioner Mills and Associates. Boston College, Newton, Massachusetts.

Harris, L., & Associates. (1985). *Public attitudes about sex education, family planning and abortion in the United States.* New York: Louis Harris & Associates.

Hernstein, R. J., & Murray, C. A. (1996). *The bell curve: Intelligence and class structure in American life.* New York: Simon & Schuster.

Hill, P., Foster, G., & Gendler, T. (1990, August). *High schools with character.* New York: The Rand Publication Series.

Hispanic Policy Development Project. (1987, Fall). *1980 high school sophomores from poverty backgrounds: Whites, Blacks, Hispanics look at school and adult responsibilities, 1*(2).

Holland, D., & Eisenhart, M. (1990). *Educated in romance: Women achievement and college culture.* Chicago: University of Chicago Press.

Holmes Group. (1986). *Tomorrow's teachers.* East Lansing, MI: Author.

hooks, b. (1990). *Yearning.* Boston: South End Press.

Hottois, J., & Milner, N. (1975). *The sex education controversy.* Lexington, MA: Lexington Books.

Imber, M. (1984). Towards a theory of educational origins: The genesis of sex education. *Educational Theory, 34,* 275–286.

Irigaray, L. (1980). When our lips speak together. *Signs, 6,* 69.

Jones, E., Forrest, J., Goldman, N., Henshaw, S., Lincoln, R., Rosoff, J., Westoff, C., & Wulf, D. (1985). Teenage pregnancy in developed countries. *Family Planning Perspectives, 17*(1), 55–63.

Kantrowitz, B., Hager, M., Wingert, S., Carroll, G., Raine, G., Witherspoon, D., Huck, J., & Doherty, S. (1987, February 16). Kids and contraceptives. *Newsweek,* pp. 54–65.

Karp, S. (1993). Many pieces to the detracking puzzle. *Rethinking Schools, 8,* 16–17.

Karp, S. (1995). Trouble over the rainbow. In D. Levine, R. Lowe, B. Peterson, & R. Tenorio, *Rethinking schools: An agenda for change* (pp. 23–36). New York: The New York Press.

Katz, S. (1996). Where the streets cross the classroom: A study of Latino students' perspectives on cultural identity in city schools and neighborhood gangs. *Bilingual Research Journal, 20,* 603–631.

Keith, M., & Pile, S. (1993). *Place and the politics of identity.* New York: Routledge.

Kelly, G. (1986). *Learning about sex.* Woodbury, NY: Barron's Educational Series.

Kelly, G. P., & Nihlen, A. S. (1982). Schooling and the reproduction of patriarchy. In M. Apple (Ed.), *Cultural and economic reproduction in education* (pp. 162–180). Boston: Routledge & Kegan Paul.

Kirby, D. (1985). *School-based health clinics: An emerging approach to improving adolescent health and addressing teenage pregnancy.* Washington, DC: Center for Population Options.

Kirby, D. (1997). *No easy answers: Recent findings on programs to reduce teen pregnancy.* Washington DC: The National Campaign to Prevent Teen Pregnancy, as cited in Wilcox (1998).

Kirby, D., & Scales, P. (1981, April). An analysis of state guidelines for sex education instruction in public schools. *Family Relations*, pp. 229–237.

Kohn, A. (1997). How not to teach values: A critical look at character education. *PhiDeltaKappan, 78*, 429–439.

Koop, C. E. (1986). *Surgeon General's report on Acquired Immune Deficiency Syndrome.* Washington, DC: Office of the Surgeon General.

Koop's AIDS stand assailed. (1987, March 15). *New York Times*, p. A25.

Kozol, J. (1991). *Savage inequalities: Children in America's schools.* New York: Crown.

Kozol, J. (2001). *Ordinary resurrections: Children in the years of hope.* New York: Harper Perennial.

Kress, H. (1997). *Bracing for diversity: A study of white, professional, middle class male and female student identity in a U.S. suburban public high school.* Unpublished doctoral dissertation, SUNY Buffalo, New York.

Ladson-Billings, G. (1994). *The dreamkeepers: Successful teachers of African American children.* San Francisco: Jossey-Bass.

Ladson-Billings, G. (2000, May). Fighting for our lives. In *Journal of Teacher Education, 51*(3), 206–214.

Lather, P. (1991). *Getting smart.* New York: Routledge.

Leo, J. (1986, November 24). Sex and schools. *Time*, pp. 54–63.

Lightfoot, S. (1978). *Worlds apart.* New York: Basic Books.

Lombardo, S. (2000). *Ties that bind: Irish (Americans) in the spaces of an Irish community center: An ethnography.* Unpublished doctoral dissertation, SUNY Buffalo, New York.

Lorde, A. (1980, August). *Uses of the erotic: The erotic as power.* Paper presented at the Fourth Berkshire Conference on the History of Women, Mt. Holyoke College, Northampton, Massachusetts.

MacKinnon, C. (1983). Complicity: An introduction to Andrea Dworkin's "Abortion," Chapter 3, "Right-Wing Women." *Law and Inequality, 1*, 89–94.

Manners, J. (1998). Repackaging segregation? A history of the magnet school system in Montclair, New Jersey. *Race Traitor, 8*, 51–97.

Markandaya, K. (1954). *Nectar in a sieve.* New York: J. Day Company.

Marsiglio, W., & Mott, F. (1986). The impact of sex education on sexual activity, contraceptive use and premarital pregnancy among American teenagers. *Family Planning Perspectives, 18*(4), 151–162.

Marusza, J. (1998). Canal town youth: Constructing poor white identities in the spaces of a post- industrial urban community. Unpublished doctoral dissertation, SUNY Buffalo, New York.

Matsuda, M. (1998). McCarthyism, the internment, and the contradictions of power. *Boston College Law Review, 40*(1), 9–36.

McCarthy, C. (1990). *Race and curriculum.* New York: Falmer Press.

McCarthy, C., & Apple, M. (1988). Race, class and gender in American educational research: Toward a nonsynchronous parallelist position. In L. Weis (ed.), *Class, race and gender in American education* (pp. 9–42). Albany: State University of New York Press.

McLaren, P. (1991). Schooling the postmodern body. In H. Giroux (Ed.), *Postmodernism, feminism and cultural politics* (pp. 144–47). Albany: State University of New York Press,.

McNeil, L. (1981). Negotiating classroom knowledge: Beyond achievement and socialization. *Curriculum Studies, 13*, 313–328.

McNeil, L. (1986). *Contradictions of control: School structure and school knowledge.* New York: Routledge & Kegan Paul.

McNeil, L. (2000). Creating new inequalities: Contradictions of reform. *Phi Delta Kappan, 81*(10), 728–734.

McRobbie, A. (1978). Working class girls and the culture of femininity. In Women's Studies Group (ed.), *Women take issue* (pp. 96–108). London: Hutchinson.

Mecklenburg, M. E., & Thompson, P. G. (1983). The adolescent family life program as a prevention measure. *Public Health Reports, 98*, 21–29, as cited in Wilcox (1998).

Meier, D. (2000). Changing the odds. In E. Clinchy (Ed.), *Creating new schools: How small schools are changing American education.* New York: Teachers College Press. Original work published 1998.

Meier, D. (1996). *The power of their ideas: Lessons for America from a small school in Harlem.* Boston: Beacon Press.

Melton, S., & Russo, N. (1987). Adolescent abortion. *American Psychologist, 42*, 69–83.

Michelson, R. A., Smith, S., & Oliver, M. (1993). Breaking through the barriers: African-American job candidates and Academic hiring process. In L. Weis & M. Fine (Eds.), *Beyond silenced voices* (pp. 9–24). Albany: State University of New York Press.

Militarism Resource Project. (1985). *High school military recruiting: Recent developments.* Philadelphia.

Moore, D. R., & Davenport, S. (1989). *The new improved sorting machine*. Chicago: Designs for Change.

Morton-Christmas, A. (1999). *An ethnographic study of an African American Pentecostal-Holiness church in the 1900s: An exploration of free space, empowerment, and alternative education*. Unpublished doctoral dissertation, State University of New York at Buffalo.

Moses, R., & Cobb, C. (2001). *Radical equations with math*. Boston: Beacon Press.

Musick, J. (1993). *Young, poor and pregnant: The psychology of teenage motherhood*. New Haven: Yale University Press.

National Research Council. (1987). *Risking the future: Adolescent sexuality, pregnancy and child-bearing* (Vol. 1). Washington, DC: National Academy Press.

New York City Board of Education. (1984). *Family living curriculum including sex education. Grades K through 12*. New York: New York City Board of Education, Division of Curriculum and Instruction.

New York State Department of Education. (1985). Memo from Dennis Hughes, State Administrator on High School Equivalency Programs. December 4, 1984. Albany, New York.

Nieto, S. (1996). *Affirming diversity: The sociopolitical context of multicultural education*. (2nd ed.) New York: Longman.

Noddings, N. (1986). Fidelity in teaching, teacher education, and research for teaching. *Harvard Educational Review, 56*, 496–510.

No racism found in Teaneck schools. (1998, June 24). *The Bergen Record*, p. B2.

Oakes, J. (1985). *Keeping track: How schools structure inequality*. New Haven, CT: Yale University Press.

Oakes, J., Wells, A., Yonezawa, S., & Ray, K. (1997). Equity lessons from detracking schools. In A. Hargreaves (Ed.), *Rethinking educational change with heart and mind* (pp. 43–72). Alexandria, VA: Association for Supervision and Curriculum Development.

Ogbu, J. (1974). *The next generation: An ethnography of education in an urban neighborhood*. New York: Academic Press.

Ogbu, J. (1978). *Minority education and caste: The American system in cross-cultural perspective*. New York: Academic Press.

Ogbu, J. (1988). Class Stratification, race stratification and schooling. In L. Weis (Ed.), *Class, race and gender in American education* (pp. 163–182). Albany: State University of New York Press.

Oldenburg, R. (1989). *The great good place*. New York: Paragon House.

Omolade, B. (1983). Hearts of darkness. In A. Snitow, C. Stansell, & S. Thompson (Eds.), *Powers of desire* (pp. 350–367). New York: Monthly Review Press.

Orfield, G., Easton, S., & The Harvard Project. (1996). *Dismantling desegregation.* New York: New Press.

Ormond, A. (2002, January). Voice of Maori youth: The other side of silence. In M. Fine & L. Harris (Ed.), *International Journal of Critical Psychology, Under the Covers: Theorizing the politics of counter stories, 4*(2), 49–60.

Perlez, J. (1986a, June 24). On teaching about sex. *New York Times,* p. C1.

Perlez, J. (1986b, September 24). School chief to ask mandatory sex education. *New York Times,* p. A36.

Petchesky, R. (1984). *Abortion and woman's choice.* New York: Longman.

Philadelphia School District. (1986). Sex education curriculum. Draft.

Polit, D., Kahn, J., & Stevens, D. (1985). *Final impacts from Project Redirection.* New York: Manpower Development Research Center.

Powell, L. (1997). The achievement knot." In M. Fine, L. Weis, L. Powell, & M. Wong (Eds.), *Off white* (pp. 3–12). New York: Routledge.

Public Agenda. (1998). *Time to move on: African American and White parents set an agenda for public schools.* New York: Public Agenda Foundation.

Public/Private Ventures. (1987, April). *Summer training and education program.* Philadelphia: Author.

Reichart, M. (2000). Disturbances of difference: Lessons from a boys' school. In L. Weis & M. Fine (Eds.), *Construction sites* (pp. 259–273). New York: Teachers College Press.

Reproductive Freedom Project. (1986). *Parental consent laws on abortion: Their catastrophic impact on teenagers.* New York: American Civil Liberties Union.

Rich, A. (1979). *On Lies, secrets and silence.* New York: Norton Books.

Rohter, L. (1985, October 29). School workers shown AIDS film. *New York Times,* p. B3.

Rosen, H. (1986). The importance of story. *Language Arts, 63,* 226–237.

Rubin, G. (1984). Thinking sex: Notes for a radical theory of the politics of sex. In C. Vance (Ed.), *Pleasure and danger* (pp. 267–319). Boston: Routledge & Kegan Paul.

Ryan, W. (1971). *Blaming the victim.* New York: Vintage.

Sapon-Shevin, M. (1993). Gifted education and the protection of privilege: Breaking the silence, opening the discourse. L. Weis, & M. Fine (Eds.), *Beyond Silenced Voices* (pp. 25–44). Albany: State University of New York Press.

Sapon-Shevin, M. (1994). *Playing favorites: Gifted education and the disruption of community.* Albany: State University of New York Press.

Sawicki, J. (1991). *Disciplining Foucault.* New York: Routledge.

Scales, P. (1981). Sex education and prevention of teenage pregnancy: An overview of policies and programs in the United States. In T. Ooms (Ed.),

Teenage pregnancy in a family context: Implications for policy (pp. 213–253). Philadelphia: Temple University Press.

Schlafly, P. (1986). Presentation on women's issues. American Dreams Symposium, Indiana University at Pennsylvania, Indiana, PA.

Schor, I. (1980). *Critical teaching and everyday life.* Boston: South End Press.

Sedgwick, E. (1990). *Epistemology of the closet.* Berkeley: University of California Press.

Selected group to see original AIDS tape. (1987, January 29). *New York Times,* p. B4.

Sizer, T. (1985). Horace's compromise: The dilemma of the American high school. Boston: Houghton Mifflin.

Sleeter, C., & Grant, C. (1994). Making choices for multicultural education: Five approaches to race, class, and gender. New York: Maxwell Macmillan International.

Smith-Rosenberg, C. (1978). Sex as symbol in Victorian purity: An ethnohistorical analysis of Jacksonian America. *American Journal of Sociology, 84,* 212–247.

Snitow, A., Stansell, C., & Thompson, S. (Eds.). (1983). *Powers of desire.* New York: Monthly Review Press.

Solomon, R. P. (1992). *Black resistance in high school: Forging a separatist culture.* Albany: State University of New York Press

Sonnenstein, F., & Pittman, K. (1984). The availability of sex education in large city school districts. *Family Planning Perspectives, 16*(1), 19–25.

Sophocles. (1984). *The three Theban plays* (R. Fagles & B.M.W. Knox, Trans.). New York: Penguin.

St. Paul Maternity and Infant Care Project. (1985). *Health services project description.* St. Paul, MN: Author.

Steele, S. (1991). *The content of our character: A new vision of race in America.* New York: HarperPerennial.

Steinbeck, J. (1937). *Of mice and men.* New York: Modern Library.

Strong, B. (1972). Ideas of the early sex education movement in America, 1890–1920. *History of Education Quarterly, 12,* 129–161.

Taylor, W. L., Piche, D., & Trent, W. (Eds.). (1997). The role of social science in school desegregation efforts: The St. Louis example. *Journal of Negro Education, 66,* 153–161.

Thompson, S. (1983). Search for tomorrow: On feminism and the reconstruction of teen romance. In A. Snitow, C. Stansell, & S. Thompson (Eds.), *Powers of desire* (pp. 367–384). New York: Monthly Review Press.

Tobier, E. (1984). *The changing face of poverty: Trends in New York City's population in poverty, 1960–1990.* New York: Community Service Society.

Torres, A., & Forest, J. (1985). Family planning clinic services in the United States, 1983. *Family Planning Perspectives, 17*(1), 30–35.

Trudell, B. N. (1993). *Doing sex education: Gender politics and schooling.* New York: Routledge.

U.S. Commission on Civil Rights. (1982). *Unemployment and underemployment among Blacks, Hispanics and women.* Washington, DC: Government Printing Office.

U.S. Department of Labor. (1983). *Time of change: 1983 handbook of women workers.* Washington, DC: Government Printing Office.

Valli, L. (1986). *Becoming clerical workers.* Boston: Routledge & Kegan Paul.

Vance, C. (1984). *Pleasure and danger.* Boston: Routledge & Kegan Paul.

Wallis, V. (1994). *Two old women.* New York: HarperCollins.

Wasley, P., Fine, M., Powell, L., King, S., Holland, N., & Gladden, M. (2000). *Small schools, great strides: The small school study of Chicago.* New York: Bank Street College.

Weeks, J. (1985). *Sexuality and its discontents.* London: Routledge & Kegan Paul.

Weis, L. (1985). *Between two worlds: Black students in an urban community college.* Boston: Routledge & Kegan Paul.

Weis, L. (1990). *Working class without work: High school students in a de-industrializing economy.* New York: Routledge.

Weis, L. (2000). Learning to speak out in an abstinence-based sex education group: Gender and race work in an urban magnet school. *Teachers College Record, 102*(3), 620–650.

Weis, L., & Carbonell-Medina, D. (1998). Learning to speak out in an abstinence-based sex education group: Gender and race work in an urban magnet school. *Teachers College Record, 102*(3), 620–650.

Weis, L., & Fine, M. (1993). *Beyond silenced voices.* Albany: State University of New York Press.

Weis, L., & Fine, M. (1996). Narrating the 1980s and 1990s: Voices of poor and working class white and African American men. *Anthropology and Education Quarterly, 27*, 493–516.

Weis, L., & Fine, M. (1998). What we as educators need to know about domestic violence. *The High School Journal, 81*(2), 55–68.

Weis, L., & Fine, M. (Eds.). (2000). *Construction sites: Excavating race, class, and gender among urban youth.* New York: Teachers College Press.

Weis, L., Fine, M., Bertram, C., Proweller, A., & Marusza, J. (1998). I've slept in clothes long enough: Excavating the sounds of domestic violence among women in the white working class. *Urban Review, 30*(1), 1–27.

Weis, L., Marusza, J., & Fine, M. (1998). Out of the cupboard: Kids, domestic violence and schools. *British Journal of Sociology of Education, 19*(1), 53–74.

Weis, L., Proweller, A., & Centrié, C. (1997). Reexamining "A Moment in History": Loss of privilege inside white working class masculinity in the

1990s. In M. Fine, L. Weis, L. Powell, & M. Wong (Eds.), *Off white*. New York: Routledge.

Weitz, R. (1984). What price independence?: Social reactions to lesbians, spinsters, widows and nuns. In J. Freeman (Ed.), *Women: A feminist perspective* (3rd ed.). Palo Alto, CA: Mayfield.

Wells, A., & Serna, I. (1996). The politics of culture: Understanding local political resistance to detracking in racially mixed schools. *Harvard Educational Review, 66*, 93–118.

Werner, L. (1987, November 14). U.S. report asserts administration halted liberal "anti-family agenda." *New York Times*, p. A12.

Wexler, P. (1983). *Critical social psychology*. Boston: Routledge & Kegan Paul.

Whatley, M. (1991). Raging hormones and powerful cars: The construction of men's sexuality in school sex education and popular adolescent films. In H. Giroux (Ed.), *Postmodernism, feminism and cultural politics* (pp. 119–143). Albany: State University of New York Press.

Wilcox, B. (1997). *Is abstinence-only sex education effective? An evaluation of the evaluations*. Paper presented at the meeting of the American Psychological Association, Chicago.

Wilcox, B. (1998). Sexual obsessions: Public policy and adolescent girls. Mimeo. To appear in N. Johnson, M. Roberts, & J. Worell (Eds.), *Beyond appearances: A new look at adolescent girls*. Washington DC: American Psychological Association.

Willis, P. (1977). *Learning to labor*. Westmead, England: Saxon House Press.

Young, A. (1983). *Youth labor force marked turning point in 1982*. Washington, DC: U.S. Department of Labor, Bureau of Labor Statistics.

Young, M.F.D. (1971). An approach to the study of curricula as socially organized knowledge. In M.F.D. Young (ed.), *Knowledge and control*. London: Collier-Macmillan.

Zabin, L., Hirsch, M., Smith, E., Streett, R., & Hardy, J. (1986). Evaluation of a pregnancy prevention program for urban teenagers. *Family Planning Perspectives, 18*(3), 119–126.

Zelnick, M., & Kim, Y. (1982). Sex education and its association with teenage sexual activity, pregnancy and contraceptive use. *Family Planning Perspectives, 14*(3), 117–126.

Zorn, J. (1982, March). Black English and the King decision. *College English, 44*, 3.

Index

About the Contributors

Bernadette Anand is a professor of urban education at Bank Street College. She is the former principal of the Renaissance School.

Doris A. Carbonell-Medina, originally from Brooklyn, New York, is a civil rights attorney, community advocate, and trainer in diversity and affirmative action. She received a Bachelor's degree in Political Science and Nonviolent Conflict and Change from Syracuse University and obtained a Juris Doctor from the State University of New York at Buffalo Law School. Formerly a staff attorney with Prisoners Legal Services of New York and community educator for Womanfocus, a program of Preventionfocus Inc., she currently serves as the community relations advocate for the Commission on Citizens' Rights & Community Relations for the City of Buffalo. She is a recipient of the Buffalo Business First 2001 Forty under 40 Award.

Michelle Fine is a distinguished professor of Education at the City University of New York Graduate Center. Her recent books include *Construction Sites* (with Lois Weis; Teachers College Press), *The Unknown City* (with Lois Weis), *Off White* (with Lois Weis, Linda Powell, and Mun Wong), and *Becoming Gentlemen* (with Lani Guinier).

Carlton Jordan is a senior research associate at Education Trust (Washington, DC), and a former high school teacher.

Dana Sherman is a middle school teacher.

Lois Weis is professor of Sociology of Education at the University of Buffalo, State University of New York. She is the author and/or editor of numerous books and articles on the subject of social class, race, gender, and schooling. Her most recent publications include *Construc-*

tion Sites (with Michelle Fine; Teachers College Press), *The Unknown City* (with Michelle Fine), *Working Class Without Work: High School Students in a De-Industrializing Economy, Beyond Silenced Voices* (with Michelle Fine), *Beyond Black and White* (with Maxine Seller), and *Off White* (with Michelle Fine, Linda Powell, and Mun Wong). She sits on numerous editorial boards and is a former editor of *Educational Policy.*